MODERN POLITICAL ANALYSIS

**PRENTICE HALL FOUNDATIONS OF MODERN POLITICAL
SCIENCE SERIES**

Robert A. Dahl, Editor

MODERN POLITICAL ANALYSIS

FIFTH EDITION

Robert A. Dahl

Yale University

Prentice Hall, Englewood Cliffs, New Jersey 07632

Library of Congress Cataloging-in-Publication Data

Dahl, Robert Alan.
    Modern political analysis / Robert A. Dahl. -- 5th ed.
        p.   cm. -- (Prentice-Hall foundations of modern political
    science series)
    ISBN 0-13-595406-1
    1. Power (Social sciences) 2. Political science.   I. Title.
    II. Series.
    JC330.D34 1991
    320--dc20   89-28463
                                                                CIP

Editorial/production supervision
  and interior design: *Mary Kathryn Leclercq*
Cover design: *Patricia Kelly*
Manufacturing buyer: *Robert Anderson*

PRENTICE HALL FOUNDATIONS OF MODERN POLITICAL
    SCIENCE SERIES
Robert A. Dahl, Editor

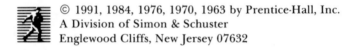

© 1991, 1984, 1976, 1970, 1963 by Prentice-Hall, Inc.
A Division of Simon & Schuster
Englewood Cliffs, New Jersey 07632

Printed in the United States of America
10   9   8   7   6

ISBN   0-13-595406-1

Prentice-Hall International (UK) Limited, *London*
Prentice-Hall of Australia Pty. Limited, *Sydney*
Prentice-Hall Canada Inc., *Toronto*
Prentice-Hall Hispanoamericana, S.A., *Mexico*
Prentice-Hall of India Private Limited, *New Delhi*
Prentice-Hall of Japan, Inc., *Tokyo*
Simon & Schuster Asia Pte. Ltd., *Singapore*
Editora Prentice-Hall do Brasil, Ltda., *Rio de Janeiro*

CONTENTS

PREFACE

In preparing this fifth edition of *Modern Political Analysis,* which by some margin is the most comprehensive revision I have undertaken, I have been particularly attentive to the discussion of power and influence. That discussion has been a pivotal feature of the book from the first edition onward. The original presentation naturally reflected my understanding and interpretation, as of that period, of this persistently difficult matter. Although a good deal of what I wrote then has, I think, stood the test of time, since then much noteworthy work on the subject has appeared, some of it critical of my original formulation. In the subsequent editions I attempted to incorporate relevant aspects of the ongoing scholarly arguments and discussions. Yet I came to feel increasingly that ad hoc modifications were inadequate and that a more fundamental recasting was necessary.

I had also come to believe that the previous presentation was defective in another respect. Given that most readers of this book, who are mainly students, must necessarily bring to it a rather limited experience with the complex world of power and influence, I concluded that my presentation was too abstract. Since readers were expected to interpret the abstractions with understanding grounded in experience, I came to fear that for many the abstractions might remain just that—abstractions. In preparing this edition, therefore, I have written a new chapter—Chapter 2—that provides descriptions of people in situations of power, including people at or near the nadir of power at one extreme and at the apex at the other. I invite the reader to attempt, difficult as it may be, to enter imaginatively into the experiences of those people. I hope that as a result the abstractions will be clothed with richer meanings.

In addition to recasting the sections on power and influence, I have given greater emphasis to the important differences between democratic and nondemocratic systems (Chapter 7) and to some of the factors that help to explain why representative democracy exists in some countries and not in others (Chapter 8). Because of the increase in both the number of countries in the world and the amount of data available, most of the tables and figures are new. I want to take this occasion to acknowledge my debt to Michael Coppedge and Wolfgang Reinicke for research that has greatly contributed to these chapters. I also wish to thank Adeleke Atewologun, Salem State College; Thomas J. Price, University of Texas at El Paso; and George J. Graham, Jr., Vanderbilt University for reviewing the book and making helpful suggestions.

Anyone who compared this book with the previous editions would surely notice one conspicuous and no doubt overdue change. The chapter "Political Man" is now titled "Political Men and Women". Although "political man" is a venerable term in political science—it is, indeed, the title of at least two books by distinguished American scholars—and though "man" is intended in its generic meaning to include women, the word may nonetheless carry with it more than a whiff of an implication that politics, or for that matter political analysis, is a man's business. Because I also wanted to add a section to that chapter emphasizing changes in political orientations, the title seemed more than ever out of place, since women provide an important illustration of just such a change.

I am painfully aware that on everything said here there is much more to be said. From the first edition to the present, however, I have wanted this to be a short book. It would have been much easier to write a longer one. To keep the book close to its original size, when adding new parts I have usually struck out old ones. No reader will, I hope, regard this book as more than an introduction to a world of experience as complex as it is fascinating.

Robert A. Dahl

MODERN POLITICAL ANALYSIS

ONE
WHAT IS POLITICS?

Whether a person likes it or not, virtually no one is completely beyond the reach of some kind of political system. A citizen encounters politics in the government of a country, town, school, church, business firm, trade union, club, political party, civic association, and a host of other organizations. Politics is an unavoidable fact of human existence. Everyone is involved in some fashion at some time in some kind of political system.

If politics is inescapable, so are the consequences of politics. That statement might once have been shrugged off as rhetorical, but today it is a brutal and palpable fact. For whether humankind will be blown to smithereens or will design political arrangements that enable our species to survive is now being determined—by politics and politicians.

The answer to the question, "Why analyze politics?" is obvious then. We cannot really escape politics—though we may try to ignore it. That is a powerful reason for trying to understand it. You may want to understand politics simply in order to satisfy your curiosity, or to feel that you comprehend what is going on around you, or in order to make the best possible choices among the alternatives open to you—that is, in order to act wisely. Although, for most people, making better choices probably provides the strongest incentive for political analysis, human beings also tend to feel a powerful need to make sense out of their world. To be sure, anyone can

1

make *some* sense out of politics; but politics is an exceptionally complex matter, quite likely one of the most complex matters human beings encounter. The danger is that without skill in dealing with its complexities, one will drastically oversimplify politics. It is fair to say, I think, that most people do oversimplify. Of course, because some simplification is unavoidable, this book also simplifies political complexities; but it does not, I believe, do so excessively. As we shall see, trying to acquire the elementary skills necessary for understanding politics is not a simple task.

NATURE OF THE POLITICAL ASPECT

What distinguishes the political aspect of human society from other aspects? What are the characteristics of a political system as distinct, say, from an economic system? Although students of politics have never entirely agreed on answers to these questions, they tend to agree on certain key points. Probably no one would quarrel with the notion that a political system is a pattern of political relationships. But what is a political relationship?

On this question, as on many others, an important, though not always entirely clear, place to start is Aristotle's *Politics* (written ca. 335–332 B.C.) In the first book of the *Politics*, Aristotle argues against those who say that all kinds of authority are identical and seeks to distinguish the authority of the political leader in a political association, or polis, from other forms of authority, such as the master over the slave, the husband over the wife, and the parents over the children.

Aristotle takes for granted, however, that at least one aspect of a political association is the existence of *authority* or *rule*. Indeed, Aristotle defines the polis, or political association, as the "most sovereign and inclusive association" and a constitution, or polity, as "the organization of a polis, in respect of its offices generally, but especially in respect of that particular office which is sovereign in all issues."[1] One of Aristotle's criteria for classifying constitutions is the portion of the citizen body in which final *authority* or *rule* is located.

Ever since Aristotle's time, the notion has been widely shared that a political relationship in some way involves authority, ruling, or power. For example, one of the most influential modern social scientists, the German scholar Max Weber (1864–1920), postulated that an association should be called political "if and in so far as the enforcement of its order is carried out continually within a given territorial area by the application and threat of physical force on the part of the administrative staff." Thus, although Weber emphasized the territorial aspect of a political association, like Aris-

[1]Ernest Barker, ed., *The Politics of Aristotle* (New York: Oxford University Press, 1962), pp. 1, 110.

totle he specified that a relationship of authority or rule was one of its essen-tial characteristics.[2]

To take a final example, a leading modern political scientist, Harold Lasswell, defined, "political science, as an empirical discipline, [as] the study of the shaping and sharing of power," and "a political act [as] one performed in power perspectives."[3]

The areas of agreement and disagreement in the positions held by Aristotle, Weber, and Lasswell on the nature of politics are illustrated by Figure 1–1. Aristotle, Weber, and Lasswell, and almost all other political scientists, agree that political relationships are to be found somewhere within circle A, the set of relationships involving power, rule, or authority. Lasswell calls everything in A political, by definition. Aristotle and Weber, on the other hand, define the term *political* so as to require one or more additional characteristics, indicated by circles B and C. For example, to Weber the domain of the political would not be everything inside A or everything inside B (territoriality) but everything in the area of overlap, AB, involving both rule *and* territoriality. Although Aristotle is less clear than either Weber or Lasswell on the point, doubtless he would limit the domain of the political even further—to relationships in associations capable of self-

FIGURE 1-1 Definitions of Politics

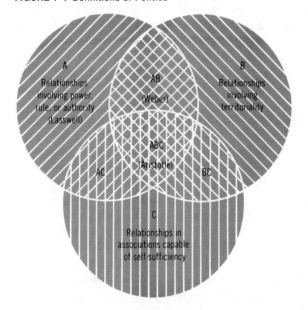

[2]Max Weber, *The Theory of Social and Economic Organization,* trans. A. M. Henderson and Talcott Parsons (New York: Oxford University Presss, 1947), pp. 145–54.

[3]Harold D. Lasswell and Abraham Kaplan, *Power and Society* (New Haven: Yale University Press, 1950), pp. xiv, 240.

sufficiency (C). Hence, to Aristotle, "politics" would be found only in the area ABC.

Clearly, everything that Aristotle and Weber would call political, Lasswell would too. But Lasswell would consider as political some things that Weber and Aristotle might not: A business firm or a trade union, for example, would have "political" aspects. Let us therefore boldly define a political system as *any persistent pattern of human relationships that involves, to a significant extent, control, influence, power, or authority.*[4]

THE UBIQUITY OF POLITICS

Admittedly, this definition is very broad. Indeed, it means that many associations that most people ordinarily do not regard as "political" possess political systems: private clubs, business firms, labor unions, religious organizations, civic groups, primitive tribes, clans, perhaps even families. Three considerations may help clarify the unfamiliar notion that almost every human association has a political aspect:

(1) In common parlance we speak of the "government" of a club, a firm, and so on. In fact, we may even describe such a government as dictatorial, democratic, representative, or authoritarian; and we often hear about "politics" and "politicking" going on in these associations.

(2) A political system is only *one* aspect of an association. When we say that a person is a doctor, or a teacher, or a farmer, we do not assume that he or she is *only* a doctor, *only* a teacher, *only* a farmer. No human association is exclusively political in all its aspects. People experience many relationships other than power and authority: love, respect, dedication, shared beliefs, and so on.

(3) Our definition says virtually nothing about human *motives*. It definitely does not imply that in every political system people are driven by powerful inner needs to rule others, that leaders passionately want authority, or that politics is inherently a fierce struggle for power. Conceivably, relationships of authority could exist even among people of whom none had a passion for power, or in situations where people who most ardently thirsted for authority had the least chance of acquiring it. Thus the Zuni Indians of the American Southwest are reported to have had a very strong sense that power-seeking was illicit and power seekers must not be given power.[5] Closer to our own experience is the not uncommon view among members of various American private organizations that those who want most intensely to head the organization are least suited to do so, while the

---

[4]In Chapter 3, words such as control, power, influence, and authority are called *influence terms*. The concept of influence is defined in that chapter.

[5]Ruth Benedict, *Patterns of Culture* (Boston: Houghton Mifflin Co., 1934).

most suitable are among those who least want the job. But whatever the evidence from anthropology or folklore may be, the central point is this: Our highly general definition of a political system makes practically no assumption as to the nature of human motives. Despite its breadth, the definition helps us make some critical distinctions that are often blurred in ordinary discussions.

(4) Our definition also deliberately ignores a quality that many political philosophers from Aristotle to the present have attributed to politics: that it is in some sense a *public* activity that involves public purposes, or public interests, or a public good, or some other distinctly "public" aspect of human life. If politics were so defined, then we should be obliged to add a fourth circle to Figure 1–1, and the domain of politics would shrink even further. But there are good reasons for not including this notion in our definition, for venerable though it may be among political philosophers, it bristles with difficulties. To begin with, this understanding of the meaning of "politics" reflects poorly how the term is used in ordinary language today, where it often refers to the self-seeking and self-promoting activity of ambitious politicians. Likewise, it surely cannot be intended as an empirical account of the *motives* that drive people enaged in politics. For to determine what motivates people requires empirical inquiry and cannot be settled simply by definition. Yet neither common experience nor systematic research seem to give much support to the hypothesis that people who engage in politics are primarily motivated by a concern for the public good. We return to the question of what motivates people in politics in Chapter 9. If, on the other hand, the notion is not intended to be either a definition or an empirical statement but an assertion of what *ought to be* the end, aim, or result of political life, then it obviously is a normative statement. But as an assertion about ends or values, it requires examination, and cannot reasonably be smuggled in simply as a way of defining politics. In Chapter 10, we return to the problems of political values.

Politics and Economics

Political analysis deals with power, rule or authority. Economics concerns itself with scarce resources or the production and distribution of goods and services. Politics is one aspect of a great variety of human institutions; economics is another aspect. Hence an economist and a political scientist might both study the same concrete institution—the Federal Reserve system, for example, or the budget. But the economist would be concerned primarily with problems involving scarcity and the use of scarce resources, and the political scientist would deal primarily with problems involving relationships of power, rule, or authority. Like most distinctions between subjects of intellectual inquiry, however, that between politics and economics is not perfectly sharp.

Political Systems and Economic Systems

Many people indiscriminately apply terms like *democracy, dictatorship, capitalism,* and *socialism* to both political and economic systems. This tendency to confuse political with economic systems stems from the lack of a standardized set of definitions, from ignorance of the historical origins of these terms, and in some cases from a desire to exploit a highly favorable or unfavorable political term like "democracy" or "dictatorship" in order to influence attitudes toward economic systems.

It follows, however, that the political aspects of an institution are not the same as its economic aspects. Historically, the terms "democracy" and "dictatorship" usually have referred to political systems, whereas "capitalism" and "socialism" have referred to economic institutions. From the way the terms have been used historically, the following definitions are appropriate.

1. A democracy is a political system in which the opportunity to participate in decisions is widely shared among all adult citizens.
2. A dictatorship is a political system in which the opportunity to participate in decisions is restricted to a few.
3. Capitalism is an economic system in which most major economic activities are performed by privately owned and controlled firms.
4. Socialism is an economic system in which most major activities are performed by agencies owned by the government or society.

Each pair of terms, democracy-dictatorship, capitalism-socialism, implies a dichotomy, and dichotomies are often unsatisfactory. In fact, many political systems are neither wholly democratic nor wholly dictatorial; in many countries private and governmental operations are mixed together in all sorts of complex ways. In the real world, politics and economics are profoundly intermixed. These mixtures not only demonstrate the shortcomings of the dichotomy "capitalism-socialism" but also emphasize the fact that some institutions and processes can be viewed as part of the economic system for certain purposes and as part of the political system for others. The point to remember is that in spite of, or even because of, this intermixing, it has proved to be intellectually fruitful to distinguish some aspects of life as "economic" and other aspects as "political."

Systems and Subsystems

Any collection of elements that interact in some way with one another can be considered a system: a galaxy, a football team, a legislature, a political party.[6] In thinking about political systems, it is helpful to keep in mind four points that apply to any system:

[6]The most extensive attempt to apply systems theory to political science is in two works by David Easton: *A Framework for Political Analysis* (Englewood Cliffs, N.J.: Prentice-Hall, Inc. 1965) and *A Systems Analysis of Political Life* (New York: John Wiley & Sons, Inc. 1965).

(1) To call something a system is an abstract way of looking at concrete things. One therefore should be careful not to confuse the concrete thing with the abstract "system." A "system" is an aspect of things in some degree abstracted from reality for purposes of analysis; the circulatory system of a mammal or the personality system of a human being are examples.

(2) In order to determine what lies within a particular system and what lies outside it, we need to specify the *boundaries* of that system. Sometimes this task is fairly easy, as in the case of the solar system or the United States Supreme Court, but often it requires an arbitrary decision. For example, what would we consider to be the boundaries of our two major parties? Would we include only party officials? Or would we also include all those who register as Democrats or Republicans? Or those who identify themselves as one or the other, even though they do not register? Or those who vote regularly for the one party or the other?

(3) One system can be an element, a subsystem, of another. The earth is a subsystem of our solar system, which is a subsystem of our galaxy, which is a subsystem of the universe. The Foreign Relations Committee is a subsystem of the United States Senate, which is a subsystem of the Congress, and so on.

(4) Something may be a subsystem of two or more different systems that overlap only in part. A college professor might be an active member of the American Association of University Professors, the Democratic party, and the PTA.

It is useful to keep these obsesrvations in mind in considering the difference between a political system and a social system.

Political Systems and Social Systems

What is a democratic society? a free society? a socialist society? an authoritarian society? an international society? In what way is a social system distinguished from a political system?

Questions like these are particularly difficult to answer because the terms *society* and *social system* are used loosely, even by social scientists. In general, however, the term *social* is intended to be inclusive; economic and political relations are specific kinds of social relations. Although *social system* is sometimes given a more specific meaning, it too is a broad concept. Thus, Talcott Parsons, a leading American sociologist, defined a social system by three characteristics: (1) two or more persons interact; (2) in their actions they take account of how the others are likely to act; and (3) sometimes they act together in pursuit of common goals.[7] A social system, then, is a very inclusive kind of order.

According to Parsons's usage, a political system or an economic system

---

[7]Talcott Parsons and Edward A. Shils, eds., *Toward a General Theory of Action* (Cambridge, Mass.: Harvard University Press, 1951), p. 55. For a discussion of the meaning and history of the concept "society," see *International Encyclopedia of the Social Sciences,* s.v. "society."

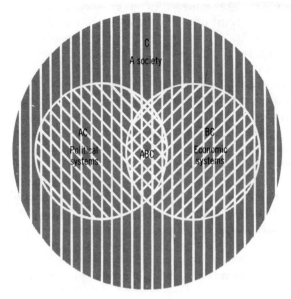

FIGURE 1-2 Society, Political Systems, Economic Systems

would be parts, aspects, or subsystems of a social system. This way of looking at the matter is illustrated in Figure 1–2, where AC represents the set of all political subsystems and ABC represents subsystems that can be considered as either political or economic, depending on which aspect we are concerned with. Examples of ABC would be General Motors, the Budget Committe of the United States Senate, or the Board of Governors of the Federal Reserve System.

Thus, a democratic *society* could be defined as a social system that has not only democratic political (sub)systems but also a number of other subsystems that operate to contribute directly or indirectly to the strength of the democratic political processes. Conversely, by definition, an authoritarian society would contain many important subsystems, such as the family, the churches, and the schools, all acting to strengthen authoritarian political processes. Let us consider two examples.

In his famous *Democracy in America* (1835–1840) the illustrious French writer Alexis de Tocqueville listed a number of "principal causes which tend to maintain the democratic republic in the United States." His list included not only the constitutional structure but also the absence of a large military establishment, equality in social and economic conditions, a prosperous agricultural economy, and the mores, customs, and religious beliefs of Americans.[8] In Tocqueville's view the prospects for a healthy democratic *political* system in the United States were strengthened enormously by the fact that

[8]Alexis de Tocqueville, *Democracy in America*, vol. 1 (New York: Vintage Books, 1955), pp. 298–342.

a highly democratic Constitution was reinforced by many other aspects of the *society*. Hence American society could be called a democratic society.

By contrast, many observers were pessimistic about the prospects of democracy in Germany after World War II because they believed that many aspects of German society were highly authoritarian and tended to undermine democratic political relations. They were mainly concerned with the wide tendency for social institutions of all kinds to take on a strong pattern of dominance and submission—the family, schools, churches, business, and all relations between government officials, whether police or civil servants, and ordinary citizens. The fact that political democracy had to be instituted in a predominantly authoritarian social environment was not particularly auspicious for the future of democracy in Germany. A number of recent observers, on the other hand, now feel optimistic about political democracy in Germany precisely because they see evidence that the authoritarian character of other social institutions has greatly declined.

Government and State

In every society, people tend to develop more or less standard expectations about social behavior in various situations. One learns how to behave as a host or a guest, a parent or grandparent, a "good loser," a soldier, a bank clerk, a prosecutor, a judge, and so on. Patterns like these, in which a number of people share roughly similar expectations about behavior in particular situations, are called *roles*. We all play various roles and frequently shift from one role to another rapidly.

Whenever a political system is complex and stable, political roles develop. Perhaps the most obvious political roles are played by persons who create, interpret, and enforce rules that are binding on members of the political system. These roles are *offices*, and the collection of offices in a political system constitutes the government of that system. At any given moment, of course, these offices, or roles, are (aside from vacancies) filled by particular individuals, concrete persons—Senator Foghorn, Judge Cranky, Mayor Twimbly. But in many systems the roles remain much the same even when they are played by a succession of individuals. To be sure, different actors may—and usually do—interpret the role of Hamlet or Othello in different ways, sometimes in radically different ways. So, too, with political roles. Jefferson, Jackson, Lincoln, Theodore Roosevelt, Wilson, and Franklin Roosevelt, for example, each enlarged the role of president beyond what he had inherited from his predecessors by building new expectations in people's minds about what a president should or legitimately could do in office. "There are as many different ways of being President," Nelson Polsby asserts, "as there are men willing to fill the office."[9] Yet expectations as to

---

[9]See N. Polsby's *Congress and the Presidency*, 3rd. ed. (Englewood Cliffs, N.J.: Prentice-Hall, Inc., 1976). Polsby compares the presidents from Franklin Roosevelt to Gerald Ford. See also James David Barber, *The Presidential Character: Predicting Performance in the White House* (Englewood Cliffs, N.J.: Prentice-Hall, Inc., 1972).

the proper role of the president also limit the extent to which they can make it what they wish—a fact dramatized by President Johnson's decision in 1968 not to seek reelection because, in effect, he could no longer play the presidential role in the way that he believed the office required.

But—a reader might ask—in defining *government* as we have just done, don't we create a new problem for ourselves? If there is a great variety of political systems—from trade unions and universities to countries and international organizations—what about *the* Government? After all, in the United States, as in most other countries, when you speak of *the* Government everyone seems to know what you mean. Of all the governments in the various associations of a particular territory, generally one is in some way recognized as *the* Government. How does *the* Government differ from other governments? Consider three possible answers:

(1) *The* Government pursues "higher" and "nobler" purposes than other governments. There are least three difficulties with this proposal. First, because people disagree about what the "higher" or "nobler" purposes are, and even whether a given purpose is or is not being pursued at any given moment, this criterion might not be very helpful in trying to decide whether this or that government is *the* Government. Second, despite the fact that people often disagree over how to rank purposes or values and may even hold that *the* Government is pursuing evil ends, they still agree on what is and what is not *the* Government. An anarchist does not doubt that he is being oppressed by *the* Government. Third, what about bad Governments? For example, do democratic and totalitarian governments *both* pursue noble purposes? That point seems logically absurd.

Our first proposed answer, then, confuses the problem of defining Government with the more difficult and more important task of deciding on the criteria for a "good" or "just" Government. Before we can decide what the *best* Government is, we must know first what *the* Government is.

(2) Aristotle suggested another possibility: *The* Government is distinguished by the character of the association to which it pertains—namely, a political association that is self-sufficient, in the sense that it possesses all the qualities and resources necessary for a good life. This definition suffers from some of the same difficulties as the first. Moreover, if it were strictly applied, we should have to conclude that no Governments exist! Aristotle's idealized interpretation of the city-state was very far from reality even in his day. Athens was not self-sufficient culturally, economically, or militarily. In fact, it was quite unable to guarantee its own peace or independence; without allies, it could not even maintain the freedom of its own citizens. What was true of the Greek city-states is of course equally true today.

(3) *The* Government is any government that successfully upholds a claim to the exclusive regulation of the legitimate use of physical force in enforcing its rules within a given territorial area.[10] The political system

[10]Adapted from Weber, *Theory of Social and Economic Organization*, p. 154, by substituting "exclusive regulation" for "monopoly" and "rules" for "its order."

made up of the residents of that territorial area and the Government of the area is a *State*.[11]

This definition immediately suggests three questions:

(1) Can't individuals who aren't Government officials ever legitimately use force? What about parents who spank their children? The answer is, of course, that the Government of a State does not necessarily *monopolize* the use of force, but it has the exclusive authority to set the limits within which force may legitimately be used. The Governments of most States permit private individuals to use force in some circumstances. For example, although many Governments forbid cruel or excessive punishment of children, most permit parents to spank their own offspring. Boxing is permitted in many countries.

(2) What about criminals who go uncaught? After all, no country is free of assault, murder, rape, and other forms of violence, and criminals sometimes escape the law. The point is, however, that the claim of the Government of the State to regulate violence and force is successfully upheld, in the sense that few people would seriously contest the exclusive right of the State to punish criminals. Although criminal violence exists, it is not legitimate.

(3) What about circumstances of truly widespread violence and force, such as civil war or revolution? In this case no single answer will suffice. During some periods, no State may exist at all, since no government is capable of upholding its claim to the exclusive regulation of the legitimate use of physical force. Several governments may contest for the privilege over the same territory as was the case in Lebanon following the outbreak of religious wars in 1975. Or what was formerly a territory ruled by the Government of one State may now be divided and ruled by the Governments of two or more States, with gray stateless areas where they meet.

We can be reasonably sure of one thing: When large numbers of people in a particular territory begin to doubt or deny the claim of the Government to regulate force, then the existing State is in peril of dissolution.

[11]Capitalized here to avoid confusion with constituent states in federal systems.

TWO
DESCRIBING INFLUENCE

In the last chapter a political system was defined as any persistent pattern of human relationships that involves, to a significant extent, control, influence, power, or authority. But what do these terms—control, influence, power, authority—*mean?*

What these terms mean is, as we shall see, elusive and complex.[1] Neither in ordinary language nor in political science do people agree on how to use these terms. Like other people, in their effort to capture important differences, political scientists use a variety of different words: control, power, influence, authority, persuasion, might, force, coercion, and so on. Like others, however, political scientists frequently do not define these terms; and when they do, they do not necessarily define them in the same way. One writer's "influence" is another's "power."

For the time being, I am going to use terms like these—"influence terms," we might call them—without attempting to define them. I want to

---

[1]The problem is not unique to political science. Physicists "define the physical meaning of the mathematical quantities t, x, F, m by means of words which are available in the English vernacular: time, body, force, etc. But are we sure what these words mean?" two physicists ask. "Every student of the empirical foundations of classical mechanics becomes aware of the difficult of defining them unambiguously." (From "A Midrash Upon Quantum Mechanics," *Science News* 132 (July 11, 1987), p. 26.)

postpone my discussion of definitions and concepts in order to plunge directly into the world of power by considering a few of the seemingly infinite number of possible shapes and forms in which power and its cousins display themselves. After we have considered some cases, we can more easily turn to the task of clarifying the meaning of influence terms.

EXAMPLES: FROM THE LEAST TO THE MOST

Suppose we begin with examples of utter or extreme powerlessness. Since this extreme condition is, happily, remote from the experience of most of us, I am going to ask the reader to attempt to enter imaginatively and sympathetically into the situation of the persons I describe.

Can you imagine, for example, what utter powerlessness might be like? A recent account of the settlement of Australia provides us with one description of human beings about as close to the zero position of control over their lives as it may be possible for a living person to reach.[2] From 1787 to 1868 the government of Great Britain exported some 160,000 convicts to Australia. Although the crime for which these convicts were convicted was often no more serious than petty stealing, their treatment was appalling. At one site in Tasmania,

> At 6 a.m., the convicts were herded into boats and ferried to the mainland to cut timber. The Settlement had no draft animals, because horses and bullocks rarely survived the voyage from Hobart and, in any case, there was not enough grass there to feed them. So the ponderous trunks, some weighing twelve tons, had to be hauled down a crude corduroy slipway of logs, known as a "pine-road," laid on the forest floor. At the tideline, the logs—sometimes a hundred at a time—were chained together in rafts and towed behind whaleboats across the harbor to the sawpits. When they got the raft back to Sarah Island, the worst part of the prisoners' work began: grappling the logs ashore with hand-spikes, struggling for hours up to their waists in icy water . . .
>
> The convict's daily ration was 1 pound of meat, 1¼ pounds of bread, 4 ounces of oatmeal or hominy, and salt. The meat was brine-cured pork or beef, two or three years old; Surgeon Barnes noted that it often had to be destroyed "as being too bad for the convicts to consume," and that in his own eighteen months at Macquarie Harbor he himself had eaten fresh meat no more than six times.

These prisoners were at the nadir of control, the extreme of powerlessness. Also at the nadir was another group of prisoners, those in Soviet and Nazi concentration camps in the 1930s and 1940s. To help you imagine their existence, consider the account of Primo Levi, a Jewish survivor of the Nazi concentration camp at Auschwitz in Poland.[3] Levi was a rare excep-

---

[2]From THE FATAL SHORE by Robert Hughes. Copyright © 1986 by Robert Hughes. Reprinted by permission of Alfred A. Knopf, Inc. British Commonwealth/UK rights courtesy of William Collins Sons and Co. Ltd.

[3]Primo Levi, Se Questo E Un Uomo (Turin: Giulio Einaudi editore, 1976), pp. 26–27, 239.

tion. The standard fate of all Jewish concentration camp victims was, sooner or later, death. For some it was sooner. When Levi arrived at Auschwitz with a trainload of prisoners, a dozen members of the dreaded SS police moved among the prisoners asking such seemingly innocent questions as "How old are you? Are you healthy or sick?" In less than ten minutes, a group of persons made up of the sick, the elderly, women, and children had been separated from the rest. They were never to be seen again; the gas chamber was their fate.

No doubt many readers would struggle nightmarishly to imagine how they might have escaped or rebelled. Yet few prisoners at Auschwitz (or other Nazi concentration camps) ever escaped or tried to rebel. They were, Levi explains, demoralized and weakened from hunger and maltreatment, their uniforms and shaven heads made them immediately recognizable, they could not speak Polish, and when recaptured they were executed, often after cruel tortures. To intimidate the others, their torture and execution were carried out in plain view of the other prisoners; the victim's friends were treated as accomplices and starved to death in prison cells; and to initimidate the prisoners even further, all the prisoners in the entire barracks of one who attempted to escape were compelled to stand on their feet for a solid twenty-four hours.

Now try to move yourself imaginatively to a position only slightly above the nadir of control by imagining that you had been born into slavery on a plantation in the Americas, in the pre–Civil War South, or perhaps in Brazil. Your ancestors would have survived the terrible passage in the hold of a slave ship, where more often than not, like the prisoners in Tasmania and Auschwitz, they were at the nadir of utter powerlessness. As a slave, you are the property of your owner, to dispose of as he sees fit, and therefore dependent on his judgments, decisions, practices, morals, passions, feelings, and whims. To survive, you must adapt as best you can. As a plantation slave, however, you are very likely to be a notch up from absolute zero simply because, as his property, your owner has some interest in maintaining you at a sufficient level of existence to ensure that you will be able to work, and perhaps to procreate. Depending upon the owner and the country (you are likely to receive better treatment in Brazil than in the United States), you may be able to find some autonomy at work or in your slave quarters, you might even acquire some authority over others—children, family, other workers in the fields or the household—and despite strong odds against success, you might perhaps become one of the few lucky ones who escape or are granted freedom by their masters.

Not quite at the nadir of control, then. But at best only a notch above it.

Now try to imagine how it might be to exist with more autonomy and power than a slave but considerably less than a free citizen: perhaps as a serf or peasant in medieval Europe, China, or Japan, or for that matter in many developing countries today. Here are scenes from daily life in a tiny rural settlement, Jaida Arriba (not its real name) in the Dominican Republic in the early 1970s:[4]

El Rio is the small village on the jeep road, over two hours by mule or foot from Jaida Arriba. Three rivers, treacherous after heavy rainstorms, must be forded to reach the Land Rover jeeps that leave for town in the early morning hours. Packed with people, with chickens, pigs, and plaintains squeezed inside or tied on top and latecomers often clinging to the back or bouncing on the luggage rack, these jeeps are one of the few links with the outside world. The nearest doctor is in the municipal capital, San Juan de La Sierra, two hours from El Rio; the nearest city with specialized medical care, hospitals, major food warehouses, markets, and large stores is Santiago, where the jeeps arrive in about three hours. They stay for a few hours while passengers make purchases, see doctors, visit relatives, and do errands. The jeeps return late in the afternoon. Many from Jaida Arriba hike or ride back at night, arriving home at 7:00 or 8:00 P.M. . . .

I ask Melida about giving birth in the campo. She says that nine of her ten children were born here in the house with the help of a midwife. Chaguito took Melida to Santiago to have one child in the public hospital. The child was five days overdue, and Chaguito was worried. Medical attention at the public hospital was free, although Melida had to bring a wash basin, cup, and spoon. And most medicines had to be paid for or bought at a nearby pharmacy. Chaguito needed about $35 to pay travel, food, and medical expenses, and he had no money at the time.

"I went to Don Pablo's House to see if he could lend me the money, but he told me he didn't have any. Then I went to Jose's house. Nothing! Those are people who've got two or three thousand pesos, but they want to keep it all for themselves. I was desperate. But then a cousin of mine called me over. He had heard that I was having problems and he told me: 'Look, if you need money, you'll find it here.' I told him I needed thirty-five pesos. He put his hand in his pocket and he said: 'Here's forty pesos.' And afterward when I paid him, he told me, 'You can always count on me anytime you need anything.'"

Still another possibility: Think of yourself as a subject or citizen of a modern country governed by a highly repressive dictatorship—Stalin's Soviet Union or Hitler's Germany—where your life could be put in jeopardy by the merest whisper of discontent—or even an ungrounded suspicion.[5] But even dictatorships vary in their repressiveness, in the amount of autonomy, control, and power they allow to their subjects. Some, for example, tolerate a surprising range of magazines, newspapers, and other forms of

[4]Kenneth Sharpe, *Peasant Politics* (Baltimore, Md.: The Johns Hopkins University Press, 1977), pp. 6, 17.

[5]Roy Medvedev, a Russian historian, has estimated that there were 40 million victims of Stalin's repressions, of whom 20 million died in labor camps, forced collectivization, famine, and executions. The estimates were published in a Soviet weekly newspaper, *Argumenti i Fakti* (*The New York Times*, February 2, 1989, p. 1). Robert Conquest, in *The Great Terror, Stalin's Purge of the Thirties* (New York: Macmillan, 1968), had arrived earlier at the same estimate of 20 million deaths (p. 533).

written expression but clamp down on public meetings and political organization; others allow a high degree of public expression and political organization but effectively prevent people from organizing competing political parties, much less participating in free elections in which the leadership might be defeated. Following Michael Gorbachev's elevation to the leadership of the Soviet Union in 1985, not only was Stalin's harsh rule publicly denounced, but opportunities for expression, participation in organizations and the election of candidates to office, and even in opposing the existing practices and institutions were greatly expanded. Though the boundaries were changing and uncertain, as a citizen of the Soviet Union under Gorbachev you would have enjoyed incomparably greater opportunities to attempt to influence the government and your fellow citizens than you might have dreamed of under Stalin.[6]

Having tried to range imaginatively from the nadir of control, utter powerlessness, to the degree of control and influence available to a citizen of a somewhat liberalized but still nondemocratic regime, you might find it a relief to think about your power and influence as a citizen in a democratic country. But before doing so, it would be helpful if you were to reflect briefly on some positions of extraordinary power—positions at the very apex of power, about as far from the nadir of power as it may be humanly possible to get. I have mentioned dictatorships, and referred explicitly to the regimes of Stalin and Hitler. It is difficult to imagine a greater concentration of control over so many other human beings in the hands of a single person, or at most a tiny group of leaders, than has existed in several modern dictatorships. Under Stalin and Hitler, so extreme was the leader's power by comparison with all other regimes, earlier or contemporary, that a new word, *totalitarian,* was coined to name these regimes. To describe those dictatorships would take far more space than we have available. However, I do want to call attention to an arresting and important fact: Even in totalitarian dictatorships, the power of leaders was very far from unlimited. Their power was, of course, limited by nature itself. Stalin could not control the weather and its often damaging effects on Russian agriculture, nor could he make plants and animals obey the "scientific laws" set forth by a Soviet agronomist, T. D. Lysenko, whose theory was declared in 1948 by the Communist Party to be the correct and official theory of genetics. Though Stalin's ill-conceived policies helped to cause the death of several million peasants, he could not force Russian peasants to bend wholly to his will, and after a quarter century of effort, at his death Russian agriculture was still a failure. And like Hitler, Stalin could not control the actions of other major powers in the world. To be sure, at the zenith of their power, Stalin and Hitler dominated the people in their own countries and those they conquered to a degree that few, if any, leaders had hitherto succeeded in doing;

[6]Striking evidence is provided by the publication of Medvedev's article, cited in footnote 5, which only a year or so earlier would have been unthinkable.

yet they were never able to dominate the rest of the world. In 1941 Stalin was betrayed by his erstwhile ally, Hitler, and was incapable of preventing a German invasion that came fearfully close to victory. As for Hitler, in 1945 he died, probably by his own hand, in an underground bunker in Berlin, amidst the war-caused ruins of his country and the ruination of a regime that, so he had proclaimed, was to last a thousand years.

CITIZENS: FROM THE LEAST TO THE MOST

Somewhere between the nadir of power and its zenith are citizens of democratic countries. Since once again I want to postpone definitions, I am going to assume that we agree roughly on what we mean by the term "democratic country."[7]

You might be tempted to think that we can now go on to a straightforward account of the power of a citizen in a democratic country. But in fact that question is extraordinarily complex—so much so, indeed, that scholarly controversies rage over what constitutes an adequate description.

We can begin, however, by assuming that a citizen of a democratic country will be entitled to a considerable array of opportunities to participate in political life, exercise control over the government, influence her fellow citizens, organize or become a member of a variety of associations, political, religious, economic, and others, and control an extensive range of decisions about her own conduct and personal life.

Yet as everyone should know from simple observation, citizens in a democratic country do not possess equal power.

Ignore the case of children and consider adults. Take work. For most human beings in any time or place, work dominates daily life. Throughout the world, and throughout history, at work control is ordinarily arranged in a hierarchy of some kind: superiors and subordinates, bosses, foremen, workers, giving orders and following orders. Thus a worker in a chemical factory in northeastern United States is asked:

Q. Are employees ever asked their opinion on work situations?
A. Never. Never. Never. You hear a lot of rumors. And then you just see it posted up. The employees are not consulted at all, or do not have any say or any anything as far as being involved in any change. . . .
Q. When there is a decision to be made regarding work [I name some], who makes those decisions and how do you hear about it?
Speaker A: It's made way over our heads and we hear about it at the last— we don't have any say at all, if that's what you're asking me. The hourly people don't count. It's a terrible state of affairs. I see it happening every day and it's getting worse.
Speaker B: Who? Us? Listen to us? They don't know us from the fork trucks.

[7]For further specification, see Chapter 7.

They just want us to do our jobs, not make trouble and go quietly out the door. That's what I do. When I tell them something, they don't listen anyway.[8]

Safety is a major concern at this chemical plant. At meetings about safety, a few bold types speak up. Most, it seems, do not.[9]

Workers have responded to the hierarchy of control at work in different ways. At the chemical plant, many accept it, perhaps grudgingly, taking it for granted as a fact of life. An Appalachian coal miner in the 1930s expressed the helplessness of many miners in the face of the coal company's control:

> I think like any other company, they want to dominate the lives of their people. . . . The way they accomplished this was in owning everything. And, naturally, if a man worked in a coal company, and he traded at a company store, and lived in a company house, then he felt like maybe politically and socially he ought to go along with exactly the way they felt.[10]

Some rebel in the time-honored fashion, by shirking. Others rebel more openly by collective action: They attempt to form unions or press for legislation to restrain management excesses. When the coal industry collapsed during the Great Depression, among miners in the southern Appalachia:

> A mood of rebellion developed, expressed by one miner who said, "If you are a slave workin' for nothin' it finally gets old."[11]

The miners flocked in droves to a union, the United Mine Workers of America. Not surprisingly, however, their attempts to gain union recognition were fought fiercely by the coal companies, which fired union members, evicted them from company-owned housing, and denied them credit at the company stores on which they were dependent for food and other essentials. In Harlan County, Kentucky:

> Two miners were killed in Harlan on the eve of the strike. On 3 January, the second day of the strike, the NMU's headquarters in Pineville were raided by deputies. Nine organizers were jailed for criminal syndicalism, while 750 miners and supporters marched to the jailhouse on their behalf. On 4 January, Alan Taub, the ILD lawyer sent in to defend them, was himself arrested within two hours of his arrival in Pineville and jailed for eight days. Meanwhile, there was a rumour of six people killed in Gatliff, and ten more persons were ar-

---

[8]Marc R. Lendler, *Just the Working Life* (San Francisco: M. E. Sharpe, forthcoming).

[9]*Ibid.*

[10]John Gaventa, *Power and Powerlessness* (Urbana, Ill.: University of Illinois Press, 1980), p. 93.

[11]*Ibid.*, p. 96.

rested for criminal syndicalism in Bell County on 7 January. In the second week of the strike, Gil Greene, a black organizer, was arrested in Middlesboro; the two key organizers, Weber and Duncan, were picked up by the Claiborne County sheriff, were severely beaten, and barely escaped with their lives. On 14 January, a nineteen-year old organizer, Harry Simms, was shot and killed by thugs near Barbourville, Kentucky. His body was taken to New York, where over 2,000 mourners marched behind it in a dramatic funeral procession from Penn Station to Union Square. Meanwhile, in the Cumberlands, the town of Middlesboro barred any meetings of the NMU, and as late as 20 March, fifteen more of the leaders were arrested in a secret meeting in the nearby Powell Valley in Claiborne County. The local sheriff, Frank Riley, announced that he had been called in to break up an 'all night party.'[12]

After more conflict and bloodshed, confronted by the power not only of the owners but the state and federal governments as well, the miners were defeated. Yet two years later with a more sympathetic Congress and president in office, "their power situation again changed, this time through federal intervention" in the form of new legislation that protected the right of the miners to join unions and bargain collectively with the employers. Ironically, however, the UMWA itself proved to be highly hierarchical, with control concentrated in its leader, John L. Lewis, who "demanded loyalty or exit."[13]

The examples I have chosen are of persons far above the nadir, certainly not powerless, yet lacking the power to exercise robust control over crucial aspects of their lives and often unable to prevail over the control exercised by others more powerful than they. Obviously the examples I have chosen are a woefully incomplete set, and it would be a grave mistake to think that they are in any sense typical or representative. A fuller examination of citizens in a democratic country would reveal an incredible variation in the extent of control exercised by different citizens, over different matters, at different times, and under varying circumstances.

Suppose, nonetheless, we leap over these countless variations and jump all the way to the apex, to that special subset of citizens who are a country's most influential leaders in economic life, government, communications, education, science, and so on. An adequate account of these occupants of positions at the apex of power in democratic countries would be a daunting enterprise, and despite innumerable bits and pieces of an account, no fully adequate description seems to exist for any democratic country. The reason is obvious. For example, to describe only one of the positions at the apex in only one country, the American presidency, ordinarily takes a conscientious scholar a whole book. Nevertheless, for our purposes it may be sufficient to point out once again this simple fact: Powerful as those at the apex may be in comparison with all other citizens in their coun-

---

[12]*Ibid.,* p. 102.
[13]*Ibid.,* pp. 117, 121.

try, the power of each is greatly limited. Their power is limited among other things by nature; by established practices and institutions, legal and other; by the inescapable scarcity of resources; by events; and by the power of other persons, including of course other leaders, who may act singly as individuals or collectively as a group, informal or organized, and who will exist not only within the boundaries of the country but elsewhere in the world as well.

WHY ANALYZING POWER IS COMPLICATED, NOT SIMPLE

As you reflect on this mere handful of examples selected from an almost infinite set of possibilities, it will surely occur to you, if it had not before, that power and influence exist in such a great variety of different ways that any simple account must necessarily omit or distort large and important chunks of what goes on in the real world. Well, you might say after a moment's thought on the matter, so does every analysis, every science, every attempt to portray complex reality in a more or less systematic fashion. After all, if we were to try to describe the mere surface of things as we observe them, we would end up with no more than the confusing details with which we started.

In the case of power and influence, however, this comforting answer is unsatisfactory. For many reasons, power *is* complicated, and to obliterate its complexities is to misunderstand it. Let me mention (still using undefined and perhaps even inexact terms) some of the reasons why a simple analysis is unsatisfactory.

1. Distribution

A satisfactory description of power and influence among some groups of people—a family, school, church, neighborhood, business firm, union, town, city, state, country, international community, or what have you— pretty clearly requires us to say something about how power and influence are *distributed* among them. Ideally, we would hope to arrive at something equivalent to a description of the distribution of income, wealth, education, life expectancy, and the like. But for many reasons, a comparably accurate description of how power is distributed is far more difficult, and probably impossible, to achieve.

2. Groups

So far I have referred to persons. But we also want to know about how power is distributed among *groups* of persons—organizations, classes, strata, regions, institutions like Congress and the president, and so on. In the denatured language of the social scientist, we can use the term "actors" to refer to both individuals and collectivities like those just mentioned.

3. Gradations

From casual observation (think of the examples earlier) we can confidently conclude that in most societies most of the time, most people are neither at the nadir of powerlessness nor at the apex, but occupy innumerable levels, stations, and positions between the nadir and the apex. This initial complexity in the distribution of power obviously cannot be conveyed by describing the power of different actors as either one or zero, all or nothing. A distribution that classified actors simply into the powerful and the powerless, or the dominant and the subordinate, would ignore a lot of the variety that would be useful to know about. Imagine how incomplete a description of incomes would be if it were to divide income receivers into only two groups below and above a certain level; and how downright misleading it would be to describe a country as if it consisted only of multimillionaires and those dying of starvation. Surprisingly, however, some descriptions of power do make this elementary mistake, as when writers treat a division into "elites" and "masses" as a sufficient account of the distribution of power in a country.

4. Potential and Achieved Power

The power of every person is limited in crucial ways. *No one possesses unlimited power*—even leaders at the apex of power—including those like Hitler and Stalin, who quite possibly achieved the highest peak of power known to human beings. Suppose that for any particular persons—call them Alice and Bill—we try to conceive of a level or amount of power (note the undefined terms "level" and "amount") that would be potentially attainable within limits set only by the laws of nature, existing technology, and human knowledge.[14] Call this Bill's or Alice's *theoretical power potential*. Probably no one ever attains his or her theoretical power potential, not only because of limits set by existing practices and institutions, but also because of particular cognitive and emotional restraints. Even persons at the very apex do not attain their theoretical power potential. Some of Stalin's and Hitler's greatest failures, for example, were set by their own cognitive and emotional incapacities. Thus Stalin failed to foresee how Russian peasants would respond to enforced collectivization, the disastrous consequences of his killing many of his best senior military officers on conspiracy charges, or Hitler's duplicity in attacking the Soviet Union, which caught Stalin utterly

---

[14]For further references to the problem of potential and achieved power, see the appendix to this chapter.

unprepared. We can certainly imagine how a wiser leader could have avoided these serious miscalculations and thus achieved something closer to his theoretical power potential. But even wise leaders sometimes miscalculate; and they are always hemmed in to some extent by the inertia of existing institutions.

Suppose we take for granted, then, that Alice and Bill will be limited by their inability to remake all the institutions and practices within which they are situated. Call these the *institutional limits* on their power. Now think of the institutional limits suggested by our earlier examples: for the slave, the institution of slavery; for the coal miner, the institutions and practices of private ownership of the coal mines; for an American president, constitutional practices and institutions such as the Congress, the Supreme Court, political parties, elections, the economic order, etc. Within institutional limits like these, few people, if any, ever achieve the degree of power that is theoretically possible given natural laws, technology, and human knowledge. In short, some persons might try to maximize their power, but few if any ever achieve it.

5. Scope and Domain

In order to describe the distribution of power, we would need to answer the question, "Distribution with respect to *whom* and *what?*" If Bill had been a slaveowner, he would have had enormous control over his own slaves, particularly with respect to their work and living conditions; but he would not have had the same power over his foreman, a free farmer nearby, or the slaves on another owner's plantation. The persons over whom an actor has power are sometimes called the *domain* of the actor's power; the matter over which the actor has power—the "what"—is sometimes referred to as the *scope* of the actor's power.[15] It is easy to see that statements like "Bill Smith has a lot of power," which do not specify domain and scope, omit some of the most crucial and relevant information about Bill Smith's power.

6. Individual and Collective Power

The way we describe the distribution of power will vary, depending on whether the actors are individuals or collectivities. As individuals Alice and Bill may be relatively powerless, but by combining their meager resources with those of other persons—perhaps others in a similar position—they may now become members of a relatively powerful collectivity. The vote is an example. One citizen's vote in a national election is trivial, but

[15]This usage seems to have been first proposed by Harold D. Lasswell and Abraham Kaplan in *Power and Society, A Framework for Political Inquiry* (New Haven, Conn.: Yale University Press, 1950). Lasswell was one of the most creative and systematic modern pioneers in clarifying the meaning of influence terms.

the aggregate vote of a large enough group of citizens can be sufficient in a democratic country to change the elected leaders and their policies. Or consider the earlier example of the miners in Appalachia. As individuals they were hopelessly outmatched by the strength of the owners, but once their right to bargain collectively with employers was protected and they joined together to form a union, they became a formidable collective power in the coal fields.

7. Sphere of Control

Choices from an agenda.   In describing the power of different actors we need to specify their sphere of control. I can clarify what I mean by "sphere of control" by assuming that Alice and Bill are citizens in a democratic country with a market economy. The political, economic, and social structures present them with various options, among which they can choose, whether in voting, deciding what to buy at the supermarket, with whom they will play tennis on Saturday afternoon, or whatnot. These are their personal choices, so to speak, and after observing and conversing with them for a time we could describe the extent of their control over their personal choices. There are, however, at least three other spheres of control we might want to describe if we wished to provide a more complete account of their power and influence.

Agendas.   One sphere consists of the set of options for choice and decision that are available to them: their *agendas.* How much influence does Bill or Alice have in deciding what options are to go onto the agendas from which they choose and deciding what options will be kept off the agenda?[16] For example, at election time Alice can choose, let us say, between two or three candidates; but could she influence the decision as to what persons are selected as candidates? Or take a case familiar to students in American colleges and universities. Students ordinarily can choose, within certain limits, from an array of courses listed in the course schedule. But typically the decision as to what course will be offered is made not by students but by faculty members. Thus as a student or a citizen, Alice may have full control over the choices she makes from the agenda as it is presented to her, but she may have little or no control over the composition of the agenda itself.

Structures.   How much if any influence does Alice or Bill have over changing or preserving the structures that present them with their agendas? By a "structure" I mean a relatively enduring institution, organization, or practice that allocates or at least significantly influences the allocation of

---

[16]This is one of the types of power emphasized in a celebrated article by Peter Bachrach and Morton S. Baratz, "Two Faces of Power," *American Political Science Review* 56, no. 4 (December 1962), pp. 947–52.

important values like prestige, status, money, wealth, education, health, and others, including, of course, power, influence, authority, and the like. Thus structures include relatively concrete organizations like family arrangements, tribes, clans, and kinship systems, together with voting systems, political parties, legislatures, universities, corporations, and religious organizations. And they also include much broader systems such as democratic or authoritarian regimes, market and nonmarket economic orders, systems of private and public property, and so on.

If we ask whether Bill or Alice has much influence over the creation, reform, alteration, or replacement of structures like these, the answer will probably be that they have practically none as individuals and in actual practice not very much by joining in a collective action either. For most people, most of the time, structures are pretty much taken as given.

Yet some people, individually or collectively, *do* significantly influence structures. The framers of the American Constitution, for example, played a decisive role in creating certain constitutional structures within which, broadly speaking, American political life has played itself out for two hundred years. We can readily think of leaders in the twentieth century who have greatly changed the political, economic, and social structures in their countries. Among modern revolutionaries one might mention Lenin, Stalin, Hitler, Fidel Castro, Mao Tse-Tung, and Deng Xiaoping. But important structural changes have also been brought about by reforms led by elected leaders in democratic countries, such as Franklin D. Roosevelt in the United States, or in Sweden the leaders of the Swedish Social Democratic Party who inaugurated the Swedish welfare state, or Jose Figueres Ferrer, who as president of Costa Rica in 1948–49 brought about the abolition of the armed forces and thereby ended the threat of military dictatorship that has been a historical commonplace throughout Central and South America.[17]

8. Consciousness

Assuming we could describe Alice's control over her personal agenda and the control by Alice, Bill, and others over the composition of their agendas and over the structures that generate the agendas of choice and decision, an element of crucial importance would still be missing from our scheme. This is the way Alice, Bill, and others think about the world, their perceptions of the options available and the consequences of choosing one or another, in short, their awareness or "consciousness." People's perceptions interact with the structures within which they make their choices and decisions. These interactions between structures and consciousness are complex—too complex, certainly, for discussion here.

[17]Cf. Morris J. Blachman and Ronald G. Hellman, "Costa Rica," in Blachman, William M. Leogrande, and Kenneth Sharpe, *Confronting Revolution: Security Through Diplomacy in Central America* (New York: Pantheon Books, 1986), pp. 156–82.

It is important to see, however, why an adequate description of Alice's or Bill's power and influence should provide some account of their awareness. Suppose an option is open that Alice is unaware of; suppose further that it is an option she would prefer to any of the options she thinks are available to her. Let us imagine that by making a telephone call to the mayor's office, she *could* get that pothole on their street repaired; but it so happens that Alice isn't aware, or simply doesn't believe, that a simple phone call would actually produce results. Alice's consciousness has rendered her less influential than she would otherwise be; her actual influence is less than her potential influence.

Or take another and more puzzling case. The public policies Bill would like to see adopted are so unpopular that no one who advocates them stands a chance of being elected. Bill's neighbor, Charlie, is, on the other hand, the perfect embodiment of the average citizen; he stands so squarely in the mainstream that most of what he wants the government to do is almost certain to be supported by both parties and enacted. In all other relevant respects, Bill and Charlie are indistinguishable. But since elected officials are more responsive to Charlie's preferences than to Bill's, we might want to describe Bill as less influential than Charlie. In any case, a comparative description of Bill and Charlie should say something about the differences in their consciousnes.[18]

Thus Bill's and Alice's control over their personal agendas is limited by the agendas themselves, by the political, economic, and social structures that generate opportunities for choices and decisions, and by their own awareness of their opportunities for exercising influence in any of these spheres. A full account of their situation, then, would include a reply to the question, "What actors exercise influence over these spheres and thereby indirectly influence Alice's and Bill's choices and decisions?"

APPENDIX (see footnote 14)

Though distinguishing in some way between potential and actual power is clearly important in political analysis, here as elsewhere, proposed definitions and concepts vary. In their pioneering effort to provide systematic clarification of political concepts, Harold D. Lasswell and Abraham Kaplan,

---

[18]While the relevance of Bill's awareness of the available options is clear enough, how best to interpret differences like those between Bill and Charlie is less clear. The importance of taking into account an actor's relative position in the way preferences are distributed among all the relevant actors is forcefully set out by James G. March, "Preferences, Power, and Democracy," in Shapiro and Reeher, eds., *Power, Inequality, and Democratic Politics* (Boulder, Colo. and London: Westview Press, 1988), pp. 50–66. See also James G. March and Johan P. Olsen, *Rediscovering Institutions, The Organizational Basis of Politics,* (New York: The Free Press, 1989), pp. 143–158.

Power and Society (New Haven: Yale University Press, 1950), defined the *actualization index* of a pattern of values as "the degree to which the pattern approximates the potential." They went on to define influence as "value position and potential," arguing that "It is important to take both potential and position into account." (pp. 59–60) However, they defined *value potential* as "the value position likely to be occupied as the outcome of conflict." (p. 58) The definition seems to me to be inadequate, and they did not develop it further. In *Who Governs* (New Haven: Yale University Press, 1961), I had a brief chapter discussing "Actual and Potential Influence" (271–75) that indicated some of the complexities in the notion of potential influence and left it at that. Felix Oppenheim prefers not to confound *power* with *ability. Political Concepts* (Chicago: University of Chicago Press, 1981), pp. 29–31. Taking the opposite perspective, Peter Morris distinguishes between "power as ability" (an actor's potential power given certain conditions) and "ableness" (an actor's achievable or actualizable power under the conditions that actually exist). *Power: A Philosophical Analysis* (Manchester: Manchester University Press, 1988). Brian Barry provides a generally sympathetic critique of Morris's argument in "The Uses of 'Power'", *Government and Opposition* 23, no. 3 (Summer, 1988), pp. 340–53. In another approach to the idea of potential influence and power, Douglas Rae proposes a distinction between what he defines as a *global possibility* (if the actor could choose any possible configuration of regimes), a *household possibility* (if the members of a house could change any of the norms within their control), a *local possibility* (changes possible through strictly local transformations), and a *local governmental possibility* (changes possible within the sphere of local government). "Knowing Power: A Working Paper", in Ian Shapiro and Grant Reeher, eds., *Power, Inequality, and Democratic Politics* (Boulder and London: Westview Press, 1988), pp. 17–49, at pp. 35. 38.

THREE
INTERPRETING INFLUENCE

So far I have been concerned mainly with questions that might arise in an attempt to describe power and its distribution. I now turn to questions of *meaning.*

THE ABSENCE OF STANDARD TERMINOLOGY

In describing some of the important aspects of power, I have used a variety of terms—influence terms, I called them earlier—loosely and often interchangeably, without attempting to clarify their meaning. Unfortunately, neither in ordinary language nor in political science is there agreement on the definition and usage of influence terms. Like others, political scientists use a variety of words that they frequently do not define; and when they do define their terms, the definitions frequently do not agree. Although influence terms have been central to political analysis throughout history, most theorists seem to have assumed, as did Aristotle, that they needed no great elaboration, presumably because their meaning would be understood by people of common sense. Even Machiavelli, who was as fascinated by the play of power as any observer has ever been, used a variety of undefined terms to describe and explain political life. In fact, the last several decades have probably witnessed more systematic efforts to tie down these concepts than have the previous millenia of political thought. As a result there has been a considerable improvement in the clarity of the concepts. Yet it is still true that scholars disagree over the meaning of "power," one writer's "influence" is another's "power," and it is difficult to pin down precisely what we mean when we say that A has *more* power (or influence, etc.) than B.

For a moment longer, however, I am going to postpone coming to grips with attempts to distinguish among different influence terms and continue to use them interchangeably. To lend a bit of concreteness to the discussion, I shall also continue to speak of Alice, Bill, and Charlie as prototypical actors, momentarily ignoring the fact that many of the most important actors are not individuals but collectivities, and that relationships involving power and influence exist not only as unilateral relations between two actors—Alice and Bill, say—but often as complex networks of reciprocal influence among a multiplicity of actors, both individual and collective.

INFLUENCE AND CAUSATION

You may have noticed that in describing influence, power, and the rest I have used expressions like "bring about," as when A brings about some action by B. "Bringing about" is simply another way of talking about *causing* something to happen. Consequently, some writers explicitly define power and its siblings as types of causation.[1]

Philosophers have shown that the idea of causation contains more profound difficulties than nonphilosophers might suppose. But despite any reservations a philosopher might have about the adequacy of our understanding of causality, it is obvious that we cannot live in the world, and we certainly cannot live satisfactorily in the world, without acting upon it. We need to bring about certain results, such as opportunities to eat enough to keep ourselves alive, and we need to avoid bringing about other outcomes (starving to death, for example). In short, not only to live satisfactorily but to live at all, we must cause some things to happen and other things not to happen. And it is not enough for us to influence nature or ourselves; we also need to influence the conduct of other persons.[2] As I have already said, it is this sphere, social power, that is our concern here.

---

[1]This view is advanced by Jack H. Nagel in *The Descriptive Analysis of Power* (New Haven: Yale University Press, 1975) and in "The Marriage of Normative Values and Empirical Concepts: Mutual Integrity or Reciprocal Distortion?" in Ian Shapiro and Grant Reeher, eds., *Power, Inequality, and Democratic Politics* (Boulder, Colo. and London: Westview Press, 1988), pp. 73–79.

[2]What about a hermit? To exist as a hermit totally independent of other persons for all needs is surely so rare that we can ignore it. And even the hermit must have depended on others for survival during infancy.

Are we interested, then, in the totality of causal relations between Alice and Bill? Not necessarily. Suppose Alice, who is running for office, mistakenly attacks Bill's firm as engaged in illegal waste disposal and thereby loses Bill's support. We might want to call this an example of Alice's *negative* influence over Bill with respect to his political support. Although negative influence is worth keeping in mind for its occasional importance, ordinarily in political analysis what intersts us is *positive* influence. Consequently, hereafter influence terms will always refer to causal relations in which the results are favorable or positive for the actor exerting influence.[3]

CONTROVERSIES OVER THE DEFINITION OF INFLUENCE

Interests versus Desires

But favorable or positive in what sense? A fundamental issue in clarifying the meaning of terms like power is the *ends* that are to be taken as relevant. In one important view, Alice's power is her capacity to bring about an outcome that corresponds with her *desires* or *preferences*.[4] This view has been challenged by others, however, who want to base the idea of power on something they feel is more substantial and consequential for human beings than desires or preferences. They therefore argue that power should be viewed as a capacity to bring about an outcome involving *interests*. This alternative view has in turn been formulated in two quite different ways. Probably the most influential formulation is by Steven Lukes, who has proposed a concept of power "according to which A exercises power over B when A affects B in a manner contrary to B's interests."[5]

Difficulties in the Concept of Interests

Lukes's proposed definition runs into several grave difficulties. To begin with, in excluding forms of control by A that are *favorable* to B's interests, Lukes's definition is not only contrary to common usage in ordinary language, political science, and political philosophy but seems rather arbitrary as well. By excluding all situations in which A's control is not contrary to B's interests, Lukes's definition arbitrarily leaves out cases that might reasonably count as involving power. For example, suppose Bill compels his rambunctious son to play in their tiny back yard in order to prevent the child from dashing into a busy street. If we can ever conclude confidently that A is acting to protect B's interests, and not contrary to them, surely it

[3] Positive influence is sometimes referred to as *control*.
[4] For example, Nagel in *Analysis of Power*.
[5] Steven Lukes, *Power, A Radical View* (London: Macmillan, 1974), pp. 27, 34. Lukes's view was adopted by his one-time student, John Gaventa, in *Power and Powerlessness* (Urbana, Ill.: University of Illinois Press, 1980).

would be in such a case. Yet are we to say, as Lukes's definition would re-quire us to do, that Bill does not exercise power over the child?

We might get around this difficulty by ignoring B's interests and con-sidering only those of A, the "powerholder." Thus James March proposes that we define "power as something like the ability to induce others to act in a way that contributes to a powerholder's interests. . . . "[6]

But here we encounter a second difficulty in any definition that, like Lukes's, makes the meaning of an influence term depend in turn on the meaning of "interests." In the specific example of Bill and his son, the "in-terests" of the child are not greatly problematical. But just as with influence terms like power, so too "interest" has proved to be extraordinarily difficult to define, at least in any way that manages to avoid highly controversial judgments in a great many concrete cases. Is a law requiring motorcyclists to wear helmets contrary to their interests—or does it protect them? If we conclude that the law is contrary to their interests, then on Lukes's terms the lawmakers are exercising power over the motorcyclists; but if the law protects their interests, then to Lukes the lawmakers would not be exercis-ing power over the motorcyclists. Although we do not need to decide here what and whose "interests" are involved, we *would* need to decide the issue of interests before we could decide the issue of power.

The difficulty with deciding what constitutes B's interests is that our judgment would be heavily dependent on our implicit or explicit theory of interests. Although it may well be true that in applying any term to the real world we to some extent presuppose a *theory* about the world, some terms are far more theory dependent than others. "Apple" is less theory depen-dent than "atom," and atom less so than "quark." Fortunately almost every-one agrees about the theory associated with "apple," most physcists agree about the theory associated with "atom," and since the mid 1960s, most physicists have come to agree substantially on the theory associated with "quark." Like "quark," "freedom," and "democracy," the term "inter-est" is strongly theory dependent.[7] Consequently, if the meaning of power depends on the meaning of interests, we would need to agree on a theory about human interests before we could agree on whether Bill is exercising power over his son, or the lawmakers over motorcyclists. And theories about human interests are among the most controversial in philosophy, political science, and social theory.

Even cases that at first blush might seem transparently easy to decide

---

[6]James G. March, "Preferences, Power, and Democracy," in Shapiro and Reeher, *Power, Inequality, and Democratic Politices,* p. 51.

[7]Just how theory dependent is illustrated by the emergence of two issues in American politics: Does a fetus have interests that entitle it to protection, when does its interests begin, and what rights, if any, do they give rise to? Do animals have interests and rights to the protec-tion of these interests? Whatever one's answers, clearly they depend on a highly controversial theory of interests.

can on examination prove difficult. Consider the case of the Appalachian coal miners mentioned earlier. Assuming the descriptions are roughly accurate, who would contest the statement that until 1933 the mineowners, often acting in conjunction with state and federal officials, used their power over the miners (and others) to prevent the miners from gaining recognition of the mineworkers' union? But in order to judge whether a union was in the interests of the miners, or its prevention was in the interests of the owners, we need a theory of interests, both short-run and long-run. I happen to share with many others a theory (loose though it may be) from which I conclude that a union was in the interests of the miners and very likely in the long-run interests of the owners as well. But this is a highly contestable theory. One who holds strictly to classical economic theory might conclude that by imposing restrictions on competitive labor markets, unions are actually harmful to the long-run interests of employers, workers, and consumers. Again, we need not try to decide the issue here. For the point of the example is only to show how dependent the concept of "interests" is on controversial theoretical assumptions. As a consequence, if we incorporate the notion of interests into the notion of power, we virtually guarantee that except in the simplest case our descriptions of power will necessarily be highly controversial.

Advantages of Distinguishing Power from Interests

If instead we make the definitions of the two terms independent of one another, *we can still say anything we would otherwise be able to say about power and interests.* We can say, for example, that A exercises power over B in a manner inconsistent with B's interests; or we can say that A's power over B serves A's interests. But to support these assertions we would need (1) to describe the relationship (of power, influence, authority, etc.) between A and B, and (2) to specify a theory of interests pertaining to A or B or both.

Thus the attempt to define *power* by linking it with *interests* combines all the problems associated not only with one but with two highly problematic concepts.[8] This solution unnecessarily complicates the problem of analyzing and studying power. A simpler (though by no means simple) solution is to define the two terms independently. Thus without confining the notion of power exclusively to instances involving the interests either of the power-holders (March) or the subjects of their power (Lukes), one might conclude in particular cases that A does in fact employ power over B in a way contrary to B's interests (Lukes) or favorable to A's interests (March).

---

[8]March, in "Preferences, Power, and Democracy," describes some of the difficulties in determining interests, though mainly in the context of measuring interests and making interpersonal comparisons. Moreover, with only a few exceptions, as in the quotation above, he explicitly makes "interests" and "preferences" interchangeable terms. The problem with which his essay is concerned—the interpretation of "political equality"—would arise in either case.

Over What Outcomes?

In view of the objections to incorporating "interests" in the concept of power, we might prefer to choose instead to define power (and perhaps other influence terms as well) as something like A's capacity to bring about outcomes favorable to A's preferences or desires.[9] Specifying the meaning of "preferences" and "desires" is by no means utterly free of difficulty but their meaning is certainly less dependent on highly controversial theoretical assumptions than "interests."[10]

But in defining influence terms, what are we to count as relevant outcomes? In particular, should nature be included? In everyday language we speak of power over nature, controlling the forces of nature, power over animals, and so on.[11] But in political analysis the term is ordinarily used in the narrower outcomes involving the actions of persons.

Throughout the rest of this book, therefore, influence terms will refer to social control, not control over nature. We might therefore sum up our definition as follows (using "influence" as a place-holder for the whole family): Influence is a relation among actors such that the wants, desires, preferences, or intentions of one or more actors affect the actions, or predispositions to act, of one or more other actors.[12]

WHAT DO WE MEAN BY MORE INFLUENCE?

Although a causal definition along these lines seems appropriate for political analysis, it still leaves us with a major problem. In describing influence and its companions, we shall often want to say that one actor has *more* influence than another. But to say "more" implies that we have compared two or more things and have found that one is greater than another with respect to some quality. But how are we to *measure* power, influence, and the rest?[13]

[9]*Negative* power (influence, etc.) would then be the capacity to bring about outcomes inconsistent with the actor's preferences or desires.

[10]The objections to using them in defining power are not so much that they are inherently ambiguous or difficult to determine as that like tastes but presumably unlike interests, they are purely subjective states that can be manipulated by others. But if so, that manipulation ought to become a part of the description of the distribution of power (over tastes, preferences, and desires, among other things).

[11]And power, control, or influence over supernatural forces, for that matter.

[12]This is essentially a paraphrase of Nagel's definition in *Analysis of Power*.

[13]Measurement does not necessarily require an *interval* scale, the strongest form of measurement. On an interval scale the units are assumed to be equal. Examples are feet or meters for measuring distance, money for measuring prices, incomes, wealth, and so on. An extremely useful though weaker scale is an *ordinal* scale on which the units are not necessarily equal but items can be ranked as greater than, equal to, or less than others. Examples are course grades, IQ scores, the hardness of materials, measures of relative pain, etc. A valid and reliable ordinal scale for comparing influence within a particular scope and domain would be extremely useful and may be the most we can reasonably expect. If so, it will never make much sense to say that A has twice as much influence as B (over C, with respect to x). Yet discussions about influence and power sometimes imply that it can be measured on an interval scale.

What do we mean when we say that the president of the United States has a great *amount* of power? Unless we can measure power in some satisfactory way, we can hardly describe the *relative* influence of different actors in a political system, or of the same actor in different times or circumstances. Or to put the problem in another way, how can we best describe the *distribution* of influence within a system and changes in the distribution over time?

An analogy may help. Economists, census takers, and policy makers often want to know how income and wealth are distributed in a country. How great is the inequality of income or wealth among American citizens? What is the effect of taxes on the distribution of income? Is the gap in incomes between white and black workers decreasing? Between men and women in the labor force? One great advantage economists have in measuring the amount of income for different persons is the existence of money as a medium of exchange. Although money is not a perfect measure of everything we might consider as income, for many purposes what we really want to know about is income received in the form of money. Money is also a satisfactory, though not perfect, indicator of wealth. Consequently despite imperfections in money as a measure, it is extremely useful for describing the distribution of income or wealth.

But how would we go about measuring the relative amount of influence of different actors in a system, that is, the distribution of influence?

As I said earlier, a statement about influence that does not clearly indicate the domain (influence over what persons?) and the scope (with respect to what matters?) verges on being meaningless. But even within a given scope and domain, how are we to compare the amount of power possessed by different actors? If influence is a form of causation, then the amount of A's influence over an outcome should be equivalent to the amount of the outcome (B's response) caused by A's desires. As direct as this approach is, theorists have shied away from it because of difficulties in measuring the amount of an effect attributable to a supposed cause.[14] Despite these difficulties, however, the approach does illuminate thought and research for it boils down to the essential question: How much do the wants or desires of some actors effect the actions and predispositions of others? No matter what techniques one may use to arrive at an answer, if power is conceived of as a kind of causation, then surely this is the right question to ask.

Even if we could reasonably employ a quantitative measure to estimate

[14]Attempts have been made to overcome the problem of measurement, with varying degrees of success. Nagel's solution required a statistical technique known as path analysis, which in turn assumes that the variables are measured on interval scales. Nagel, *Analysis of Power*, pp. 55ff. As Nagel pointed out, however, "(t)he appropriateness of path analysis for ordinal data remains a major unsettled issue ..." (p. 27). He sought to resolve many of the difficulties in a later paper ("Recent Developments in the Measurement of Power," presented at the International Political Science Association meetings, Moscow, 1979), and more recently he has reaffirmed his belief "that we can observe and measure power in many situations, and that we can develop (and have already developed to some extent) models and theories that explain what we observe." ("The marriage of Normative Values and Empirical Concepts", in *Power, Inequality, and Democratic Politics*, p. 77).

an actor's influence within a given scope and domain, we would still face the problem of adding an actor's influence in various scopes and domains to arrive at an aggregate. How could we determine, for example, whether the president is, in the aggregate, more powerful than the Congress?

The difficulty is this: There does not appear to be a satisfactory objective method for weighing either scopes or domains. Scopes might be as diverse as, for example, foreign policy, taxation, appropriations, public opinion, elections, and so on. Domains might vary from a multitude of voters to one person who happens to be the chairman of a powerful congressional committee. If Alice can mobilize 10,000 voters in an election, and Bill can persuade the chairman of the House Appropriations Committee to support his proposal, who is more influential, Alice or Bill? It seems reasonable to say that Alice has greater aggregate influence than Bill only if Alice's influence is as great as Bill's in all scopes and domains and greater in at least one scope and domain. As our example suggests, however, real life does not always produce such neatly tailored situations. Although we might try to assign weights to different areas, weights are bound to be arbitary. If schools are given a weight of 1, what weight should be given to political nominations—2, 5, ½? At present there is no single best way of solving the problems of comparability when actors have different amounts of influence with respect to different scopes or domains.

OBSERVING AND DESCRIBING INFLUENCE: SUMMARY

Considering the difficulties in interpreting influence terms, you might begin to wonder how you could possibly arrive at a satisfactory description of power relations. The answer is that the formal ideas presented here serve as guides to observation and analysis. They constitute criteria that can rarely be met perfectly and often only crudely.

The best political observers ask essentially the questions suggested by our semantic analysis so far. For example, they may ask: What persons or groups have the greatest effect on congressional tax measures? Who tends to initiate proposals, to win others over to them, to carry them through over opposition, to veto or sidetrack the proposals of others? Why do some questions never become public issues?

Because of the obstacles to creating quantitative measures that capture enough of the richness of meaning in relationships of power and influence, the fullest accounts of real-world systems of power relations are rarely if every purely quantitative. Even the most appropriate quantitative analysis invariably requires additional qualitative interpretation in order to convey sufficient meaning to the analysis. More often, quantitative analysis is a useful and sometimes even indispensable supplement to qualitative accounts, though it does not displace them. It may seem paradoxical that the subtlety and complexity of power relations are often best portrayed in works of fiction. But at this point, that conclusion should not come as a surprise.

FOUR
EXPLAINING AND APPRAISING INFLUENCE

In the last two chapters we explored the question of interpreting the *meaning* of influence and *describing* it. Assuming then that we can arrive at a satisfactory description of a system of influence relations, how are we to *explain* what we have found? And how ought we to appraise or *evaluate* the system we have described and explained?

EXPLAINING DIFFERENCES IN INFLUENCE

In general, differences in the amount of influence that persons exercise can be attributed directly to three fundamental explanatory factors:

1. Differences in the distribution of political resources. A political resource is a means by which one person can influence the behavior of other persons. Political resources therefore include money, information, food, the threat of force, jobs, friendship, social standing, the right to make laws, votes, and a great variety of other things.
2. Variations in the skill or efficiency with which individuals use their political resources. Differences in political skill stem in turn from differences in endowments, opportunities, and incentives to learn and practice political skills.
3. Variations in the extent to which individuals use their resources for political

purposes. Of two equally wealthy people, for example, one may use her wealth to gain influence while another may use his to achieve success in business. These variations are themselves traceable to differencs in motivation that arise out of variations in endowments and experiences.

The Network of Causes

Thus some key links in the causal network might be illustrated by Figure 4–1. These links are only a part of the network of causation. Other links radiate indefinitely beyond this immediate focus. The analysis of influence is similar to other causal analysis. How do we explain a particular forest fire? If we conclude that it was caused by campers, why did the campers cause the fire? Did they deliberately set it? If so, why did they wish to set fire to the forest? If their action was not deliberate, how do we explain their carelessness? What about other causes? Were the woods unusually dry? If so, why? Shall we also try to explain the peculiar weather? Is this likely to be a long-run cycle? Why didn't the Park Service prevent camping during the dry period?

The links on which we focus attention in a causal explanation depend on our purposes and interests. Perhaps we want to understand why campers are careless with fires in the hopes that a program of public information or regulation might help. Or we may want to determine how the Park Service can prevent fire. We may also want to consider changing the weather by cloud-seeding during dry periods. If complete analysis required us to trace every cause back to its causes, with an indefinitely widening network of causes, then a complete analysis of forest fires would be impossible.

So, too, with the analysis of influence. Where we wish to bring our

FIGURE 4-1 Some Factors Accounting for Differences in Political Influence

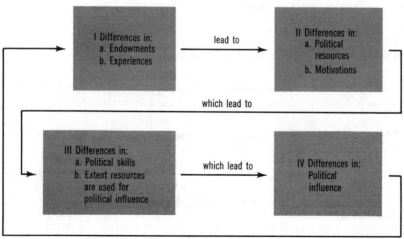

inquiry to a halt depends upon our interests. For example, if we want to explain why certain decision makers, such as the president, make the decisions they do, we could examine the effects of:

Their current values, attitudes, expectations, and information

Their earlier or more fundamental attitudes, values, beliefs, ideologies, personality structures, and predispositions

The values, attitudes, expectations, information, beliefs, ideologies, and personalities of others whose actions are in some way relevant to the decision

The process of selection, recruitment, or entry by which decision makers arrive at their positions

The rules of decision making they follow, the political structures, the constitutional system

The other institutions of the society—the economic, social, religious, cultural, and educational structures that allocate key resources

The prevailing culture, particularly the political culture

The historical events that influenced the culture, institutions, and structures

And so on.

No doubt a complete explanation of influence relations in a political system would try to describe and explain effects attributable to all these links in the chain of social causation, and others as well. Yet this is such a staggering task that it might well serve as a program for all the social sciences for generations. Meanwhile, it is important to specify the links in the chain one is studying. A good deal of confusion and controversy are produced when analysts focus on different links in the chain of power and causation without clearly specifying what effects they wish to explain.

POSSIBILITIES AND LIMITS

The bottom arrow in Figure 4–1 represents an extraordinarily important feature of influence: *Influence can be used to acquire more influence.*

Employing influence to gain more influence is surely one of the most basic themes in human history. Imagine a group of people who because of their endowments and experiences (I in Figure 4–1) live in a condition of equality in political resources, more or less (IIa). But because of differences in incentives and motivations (IIb) and in the extent to which they cultivate their political skills and use their resources to gain influence (IIIa and b), one person[1] among them gains influence (IV), which he then uses to acquire more resources (I), thus more influence (II, III, IV), thereby more political resources. . . . As an engineer might put it, here we have an example of a runaway system.

[1]Or collective actor, of course. For the sake of concreteness, I assume here that the actor is a person—and a male, as would throughout history have been the more likely case.

In a comparable runaway political system presumably one person would attain complete and total power over all the others, who would be completely and totally powerless. Let us refer to this as a system of total domination of subjects by a single ruler. Yet the examples in Chapter 3 suggest that systems of total domination are extremely rare, if indeed they exist at all. Why does the principle that influence can be used to gain more influence not lead inexorably to systems of total domination?

The explanation rests on a simple fact.[2] Exercising influence requires the expenditure of political resources. Resources are limited or, as economists like to say, scarce. Consequently, exercising influence is costly. Hence a moderately rational ruler would not commit his resources beyond the point at which the value of the benefits he expected to gain were exceeded by the costs. The *value of influence* might thus be defined as the excess of expected benefits over expected costs. If the costs of influencing others in a particular domain and scope exceed the benefits to the ruler seeking influence, then effective influence in that range or domain has no value for the ruler. A rational (or even moderately reasonable) ruler would allocate his resources among goals so as to maximize the net benefits he expects to gain. Whenever the costs of influence exceed the benefits, a reasonable ruler would reduce costs by leaving some actions or matters beyond his control or accepting a higher level of unreliability and predictability in his influence over others.

For the subjects of domination, the trick is to raise the costs and thus reduce the value of domination by the ruler. Several factors may enable them to do so. To begin with, as we saw in Chapter 2, subjects nearly always have access to some resources, however pitiful they may be. They can sometimes cooperate, combine their resources, and thus increase the ruler's costs of dominating them. Moreover, because of inherent limits on the time, skill, and resources of a single person, rulers require the cooperation and support of others, particularly in large systems. Rulers nearly always need generals, for example, and generals will command a military establishment. Except in tiny systems, therefore, the "ruler" is likely to be a group, coalition, class, or collectivity of some sort. But ruling groups seldom remain completely unified. Factions develop, and the factions contest for power. If some subjects have resources that might be thrown into the struggle for power and influence—such as an ability and willingness to fight—their help could be crucial to the victory of one faction or another.

Although this brief summary greatly simplifies the process, one could endlessly multiply historical examples showing how members of a weaker group have combined their resources, raised the costs of control, overcome domination on certain matters important to them, acquired some measure

---

[2]For a more extended treatment, see my *Dilemmas of Pluralist Democracy, Autonomy vs. Control* (New Haven, Conn.: Yale University Press, 1982) from which the following paragraphs are adapted (pp. 33ff.).

of political autonomy, and by virtue of their bargaining position even created a system of mutual controls in which subjects influence the ruler in important respects, even though the ruler remains the dominant (though no longer totally dominant) actor in the system. Such systems may and often do settle down into institutional arrangements that come to be so widely accepted, particularly among the ruling group, that they cannot be altered without great cost. In some instances, political practices may develop into a written or unwritten constitution that is generally understood to be binding on rulers and subjects alike. Thus institutionalization may significantly raise the costs of influence and reduce the resources available to rulers.

To be sure, although factors like these tend to prevent total domination of rulers over subjects, particularly in large systems, they do not necessarily prevent gross inequalities in power and influence. Certainly they do not ensure equal influence, whatever that might mean.[3] Nor are they sufficient to guarantee a democratic system, which is a rare political species that requires unusual conditions for its existence.[4] But these factors do explain why, despite the fact that influence may be used to gain more influence, systems of total domination rarely if ever exist on a large scale.[5]

FORMS OF INFLUENCE

The explanation just given employs another common though undefined influence term, domination. It is now time to make some of the distinctions I have postponed making.

To most of us, words like *influence, power, authority, control,* and *domination* suggest different meanings. Describing the chairman of his committee, a member of Congress said, "I wouldn't use the term *powerful*. I'd say *influential*. There's a difference."[6] Political description and explanation would be impoverished if we were compelled to work only with the generic meaning of the term *influence* set forth in the last chapter. For differences in influence make a difference to us.

While it would go far beyond our purposes here to clarify all the distinctions implied by common usage, I want to emphasize several of the most important differences in forms of influence.

[3]On the difficulty of specifying what we might mean by political equality, see James G. March, "Preferences, Power, and Democracy," in Ian Shapiro and Grant Reeher, eds., *Power, Inequality, and Democratic Politics* (Boulder, Colo. and London: Westview Press, 1988), pp. 73–79.

[4]These conditions are examined in Chapter 8.

[5]The term totalitarian was invented as a name for what sometimes were described as if they were systems of total domination, specifically in the Soviet Union, fascist Italy, and Nazi Germany. But powerful as Stalin, Mussolini, and Hitler were, they never achieved *total* domination of all the people in their countries.

[6]Quoted in John Manley, *The Politics of Finance: the House Committee on Ways and Means* (Boston: Little, Brown & Co., 1970), pp. 122–23.

Control

In the last chapter I called attention to the distinction between negative and positive influence and said that in political analysis we are ordinarily interested in positive influence. To maintain the distinction, positive influence is sometimes referred to as *control.*

Persuasion

Rational persuasion.   One form of influence that often is singled out as humane and desirable takes place by means of rational communication—a successful effort by A to enable B to come to an understanding of the "true" situation by means of truthful information.[7] Persuasion by rational communication (*rational persuasion*) is consistent with Kant's moral injunction that one should treat other human beings always as ends in themselves, never as means to an end. In this respect, some people might object to conceiving of rational persuasion as influence at all. Yet it is, as a few examples will show.

A physician warns a patient: "If you don't stop smoking three packs of cigarettes a day, you run a high risk of lung cancer. And you certainly aren't doing your weak heart any good either." A lawyer advises a client: "My best judgment is that if you take this to court, you'll lose." An architect apologizes: "I'm sorry, but I've costed out the house you had in mind, and it is going to cost you at least twice the figure you stipulated as your outside limit." In each case, if the client responds to the alternatives in the light of this new information, the physician, lawyer, or architect has caused the client to do something that he or she otherwise would not have chosen to do. In terms of influence, the desires of the professional have affected the client's actions or predisposition to act.

It is no accident that the examples I have chosen are all drawn from relations between professionals and clients. A professional code of conduct requires that in relationships with the client, professionals transmit only information that is, to the best of their knowledge, truthful.

Manipulative persuasion   Rational persuasion represents rational communication in its purest form. But there are many dishonest forms of communication in which there is no intention of transmitting only truthful information. Persuasion can be deliberately deceptive. Here A seeks to persuade B to act not by providing a correct understanding of the alternatives

---

[7]Akin to rational persuasion is the "ideal speech situation" and the "communicative ethics" described by the German philosopher and social theorist Jürgen Habermas. See his "Towards a Theory of Communicative Competence," *Inquiry,* 13:4 (Winter 1970), pp. 360–75. For a brief account and critique, see William A. Galston, *Justice and the Human Good* (Chicago: University of Chicago Press, 1980), pp. 41–46. For a fuller exposition, see Thomas McCarthy, *The Critical Theory of Jürgen Habernmas* (Cambridge: MIT Press, 1979), Chap. 4 pp. 272–357.

based upon truthful information but by means of manipulating B's understanding. Manipulative persuasion exists when A influences B by communication that intentionally distorts, falsifies, or omits aspects of truth known to A that if made known to B would significantly affect B's decision. Most advertising is a form of manipulative persuasion.

Unlike rational persuasion, manipulative persuasion is inconsistent with Kant's moral imperative: In manipulative persuasion persons are treated not as ends but as means, instruments, or subjects. Although manipulative persuasion usually is thought to occupy a moral standing far beneath rational persuasion, in philosophical and ideological statements great ends are not infrequently held to justify intrinsically bad means. Thus Plato recommended manipulative persuasion in order to establish his ideal Republic.[8] Political movements across the spectrum from left to right have followed Plato's footsteps. Former President Nixon and his advisers justified the great Watergate cover-up on these grounds.

Inducement   Often when A wishes to control B with respect to some scope of activity, it is insufficient for A to communicate information—truthful or deceptive—about the alternatives B supposedly confronts. An employer who warns employees, "If you go on strike, you'll lose your wages," ordinarily would be telling the truth, but the employees might nonetheless choose to strike. The employer might try to manipulate employees' understanding by dubious truth or even by outright lies: "Look, if you go on strike, you'll never get another job with this company." Yet the employer might still fail to persuade workers who believe that their wages are too low, and therefore they will join their fellow workers in a strike for higher wages. The employer might prefer to avoid a strike altogether by giving in to a wage raise, thus inducing the employees to stay on the job. The employer influences employees by changing the nature of the alternatives themselves: The employer adds to the attractiveness of remaining on the job in comparison with striking.

In comparison with rational persuasion, which is generally considered a good means of influence, and manipulative persuasion, which is widely condemned (although widely practiced), influence by means of rewards has no definite moral standing one way or another. Nearly everyone, I imagine, considers positive inducements good in some situations and bad in others. To judge whether the employer is right to offer employees higher pay not to strike and whether an employee is right to accept it, would require a thorough analysis of the situation and a social-political perspective, an ideology or a political philosophy, that would provide grounds for arriving at a judgment.

[8]G. M. A. Grube, trans., *Plato's Republic* (Indianapolis: Basic Books, 1974), lines 414d–415d.

Power.   With other kinds of influence by inducements, however, the ethical questions are more acute and direct. Suppose, for example, that an employer says: "A strike is in violation of the company's contract with the union. If you go on strike, I'll get an injunction and within twenty-four hours you'll be in jail." In addition suppose that this is a truthful statement. Whereas in the preceding example the employer changed the employee's preference ordering by adding an alternative consisting of a positive inducement, in this example the employer modifies an existing alternative— to strike—by adding the prospect of severe punishment. Influence of this kind, when compliance is attained by creating the prospect of severe sanctions for non-compliance, is often called power.[9]

Such a conception of power may have been in the minds of members of the Ways and Means Committee who denied that their chairman, Wilbur Mills, exercised "power" over them:

> Power—you mean influence? In the sense of influence? I agree with that. He's considerate. He's as considerate of the most junior member as he is of the most senior. That's why he's "powerful."
> I wouldn't use the term powerful, I'd say influential. There's a difference. I'll compare him with ... Carl Vinson. Carl had power and he used it, he wasn't afraid to use it. Mills is different. He has influence. I don't mean influence in the sense you peddle influence. It isn't "you do this for me" or on a committee assignment.... He can always bring you together. He has such great respect and influence.[10]

Exactly what constitutes a "severe" loss or deprivation is somewhat arbitrary. What a person regards as severe varies with experiences, culture, bodily conditions, and so on. Nonetheless, probably among all peoples, exile, imprisonment, and death are considered severe punishments. Therefore, whoever can impose these penalties is bound to be important. Indeed, the State is distinguishable from other political systems only to the extent that it successfully upholds the claim to the exclusive right to determine the conditions under which severe penalties—those involving serious physical pain, constraint, punishment, or death—may be legitimately employed.

[9]This accords with the definition of Harold D. Lasswell and Abraham Kaplan, in *Power and Society* (New Haven: Yale University Press, 1950): "A *decision* is a policy involving severe sanctions (deprivations).... *Power* is participation in the making of decisions.... It is the threat of sanctions which differentiates power from influence in general. Power is a special case of the exercise of influence: it is the process of affecting policies of others with the help of (actual or threatened) severe deprivations for nonconformity with the policies intended." Lasswell cites as comparable John Locke's use of the term in the *Two Treatises of Government* (1690): "Political Power, then, I take to be a right of making laws, with penalties of death, and consequently all less penalties," pp. 74–76.

[10]Manley, *The Politics of Finance*, pp. 122–23. Manley, it should be said, interprets these remarks as implying a difference between a one-way relationship (power) and a "mutual process of stimulation" (influence).

Coercion. Suppose that, in a strike situation, Carson desperately wants to go on working. His wife is ill, he has staggering medical expenses, his unpaid bills are overwhelming, he is about to sell his car and his house to scrape up cash—and the union has no strike fund. In these circumstances, Carson's preferences are, from best to worst:

1. To go on working at the same pay
2. To quit and find another job
3. To strike

But let us suppose that the labor union has been taken over by criminal elements who use the strike weapon to extort protection money from business firms. Allston, a union agent, threatens: "Carson, if you don't go on strike, and you try to go through our picket line, we'll beat you to a pulp. And don't think you can sneak off and get another job either. Your kids might just have an accident on the way to school. You're going to join the strike—or else." After thinking it over, Carson now feels that his only alternatives are, from best to worst:

1. To strike
2. To go on working (and be badly beaten up)
3. To quit (and have his children injured)

Carson is caught. From his point of view, his options are all unsatisfactory. He is compelled to do what he had not wanted to do at all because the only remaining alternatives are much worse. If he tried to explain his situation, Carson might say, "I don't want to strike but I *have* to. I have no choice. They're forcing me to do it." In this situation, a philosopher might say that Carson is coerced.

In this instance the relationship involves a particularly sinister form of power because all the options open to Carson entail severe sanctions. No matter what he does, Carson will be a good deal worse off. He is compelled to choose a damaging alternative because all the others are even worse. This is coercion. The classic case of coercion is the one illustrated by: "Your money or your life!"

Just as power is a form of influence, so coercion is a form of power. But not all power is strictly coercive in the sense just defined. If positive inducements are combined with severe sanctions to bring about the action desired, the relationship is one of power but not of coercion in the strict sense.

Physical force. Power and coercion do not necessarily require the use or threat of physical force. However, physical force, although it is an inefficient form of influence, too clumsy and costly for most purposes, is often involved in power and coercion. Despots may rule by fear, but never only by force. Even a despot needs guards, jailers, and a military that is loyal and obedient. And the despot alone cannot gain obedience from every soldier, jailer, or guard to comply by direct force.

What makes coercion effective is not the actual use of physical force, rather it is the threat to harm another by physical force if the other does not comply. The threat of force often makes coercion an effective goad or deterrent to action. The actual use of force occasionally may help make the threat credible. But if the threat must always be carried out, coercion by force becomes self-defeating. A thief may turn a live victim into a dead one, but a corpse cannot open the safe. If the great powers should every carry out the threat of nuclear war, there may be no survivors. The actual employ-ment of physical force, then, usually signifies that a policy based on the threat of force has failed.

Domination.   Political systems are sometimes portrayed as consisting only of relations of *domination* and *subjection.* Although in such portrayals these terms are rarely defined rigorously, if at all, writers who use these descriptive categories often seem to imply that (1) all power relations are highly coercive, (2) all actors either exercise power or are powerless (the amount of power is either one or zero, all or none), and (3) everyone is therefore a member of either the dominant class or the subject class. For reasons we have already discussed, interpretations of this kind are too sim-ple to account for the complex relations even in authoritarian regimes, much less in looser, more democratic systems. Because of their excessive simplification, descriptions along these lines seem to have lost favor among social scientists, although they continue to play a part in popular, journalis-tic, and propagandistic accounts.[11]

Manifest and Implicity Influence

Over several years prior to 1170, King Henry II of England had been deeply angered by certain utterances and actions of Thomas à Becket, the Archbishop of Canterbury. In late December of that year, the king ex-pressed his anger against Thomas Becket in harsh terms that four knights interpreted as a desire to have Becket done away with. Four days after Christmas they murdered him in the cathedral at Canterbury. So far as can be determined, the king had not actually ordered the knights to undertake the murder. Nor can it be determined with certainty whether he actually wanted Becket murdered or only seemed to imply so in a fit of rage. Judging

[11]This is not to say that concepts of domination and subjection could not be useful if they were carefully defined. It is only to say that they are not useful unless they are carefully defined, and they rarely are.

Henry's responsibility for the murder thus raises not only moral issues but also empirical questions (on which a moral judgment would depend).

Clearly Henry in some sense influenced the knights. Though he did not *manifestly* bring about the murder, did he *implicitly* cause the knights to murder Becket? If it was his desire that Becket be murdered, and the knights correctly interpreted and acted on their understanding of his desires, then we would want to say that Henry exercised implicit influence over the knights, and thus was morally responsible for the murder.[12]

Although observing, describing, explaining, and evaluating implicit influence presents serious difficulties, it is a highly important form of control.[13] Like Henry II, leaders everywhere control their subordinates as much by implicit as by manifest influence. Elected officials respond to the implicit wishes of their constituents, adults to infants, businessmen to consumers, governments to businessmen and other interest groups.[14]

EVALUATING FORMS OF INFLUENCE

These distinctions are important to us because of their moral and practical significance. Most of us tend to regard rational persuasion, for example, as more desirable than coercion. To make a thoughtful evaluation of the different forms of influence is no easy matter. I can do no more here than to offer a few suggestions that ought to be considered an introduction and not a conclusion to the subject.

Among the forms of influence, rational persuasion may have a claim to a unique moral standing. The grounds for such acclaim would be something like this: Because, by definition, the only means it employs is the accurate communication of information believed to be strictly true, rational persuasion is a form of enlightenment. To the extent that the information conveyed by rational persuasion is in fact true, it cannot be intrinsically harmful to the other. It may forecast possible harm: "If you do not stop smoking, you may incur lung cancer." But rational persuasion is itself intrinsically neutral: By itself it neither adds to nor subtracts from the good of

[12]A dramatic account is given in T. S. Eliot's play, *Murder in the Cathedral* (1932). It is of course the very ambiguities and uncertainties of the situation that make Eliot's play far more than an historical account.

[13]Carl J. Friedrich introduced the "rule of anticipated reactions" in 1937 to refer to a situation in which "one actor, B, shapes his behavior to conform to what he believes are the desires of another actor, A, without having received explicit messages about A's wants or intentions from A or A's agents." *Man and His Government* (New York: McGraw-Hill Book Co., 1963), pp. 201–2.

[14]Charles E. Lindblom contends that in countries with privately owned, market-oriented economic systems, business people enjoy a "privileged" position because in order to induce them to perform satisfactorily, governments must provide them with a great variety of rewards, *Politics and Markets* (New York: Basic Books, Inc., 1977), pp. 170–200.

the other. It is, however, desirable instrumentally (or extrinsically) because through enlightenment it may bring about the good of the other: Armed with knowledge acquired through rational communication, the other may now choose the better rather than the worse alternative—or, at the least, accept the inevitable.

It is no accident, then, that a notion of mutual influence based on rational persuasion lies often half-hidden in the heart of many conceptions of an ideal society. In the eyes of many Athenians, an ideal polis might well have had this quality. Influence in the assembly by gifted leaders like Pericles would rest solely on their exceptional capacity for rational persuasion. Rousseau's conception of a republic in which every citizen is morally free and yet bound by laws of his own choosing also partakes of this idea. Citizens engage in mutual, rational persuasion and accept freely the obligations created by the collective decisions taken at the conclusion of the discussion. This is an implicit ideal in a great deal of democratic thought. It is often an even more explicit ideal in anarchist thought.

Yet no large number of persons has ever interacted over an extended period of time in and outside their group without developing means of influence other than rational persuasion.

Manipulative persuasion, power, coercion, the threat and application of physical force are commonplace aspects of political life. Every State uses power internally to secure compliance with the policies of the Government. Manipulative persuasion, power, coercion, and physical force have been common in the relations among States; in international politics, war or the threat of war has frequently been used as an alternative to stalemate or peaceful adjustment. Civil wars and revolutions also involve power and coercion; each side resorts to physical force to impose its will on others. It is easy for people accustomed to relatively stable political systems such as those of Britain and the United States to lose sight of the frequency of revolutions, civil wars, and violence. Even today, in large parts of the world, civil strife, guerrilla warfare, revolutionary struggles, terrorism, violence, and suppression of political opponents by physical force are normal and commonplace political practices. It may help Americans to understand the pervasiveness of "internal war" if they remember that our Civil War lasted five years and was one of the bloodiest exhibitions of fratricide in modern history.

Although these things happen, this is not to say that they are morally justified. One might ask, then, whether anything other than rational persuasion can ever be morally justified. After all, manipulative persuasion violates a fundamental and widespread ethical injunction that favors truth over lying. Power, particularly in the form of coercion and where physical force is employed, involves the prospect of inflicting pain on another person, sometimes even causing death. Thus power may be, and coercion surely is, intrinsically harmful.

To avoid intrinsically undesirable means, one might conclude that the only morally permissible means of influence is rational persuasion. Let me call this the *absolute principle* of rational persuasion. Yet this solution immediately leads to self-contradiction unless it is universally adopted. Suppose that some persons use manipulative persuasion or coercion to get what they want. How are we now to apply the principle of rational persuasion? On the one hand, we might conclude that the principle enjoins us to use only rational persuasion in order to dissuade the violators of that principle. Yet if rational persuasion proves ineffectual, as it will in many cases, then we have no effective way of upholding our principle in practice. Alternatively, then, in order to enforce our principle, we might punish or threaten to punish the violators of that principle. But in this case we ourselves will have violated the principle.

Because of this dilemma, it appears that the absolute principle of rational persuasion never can be upheld until it is always adhered to by everyone. Consequently, even pacifists and advocates of nonviolence are rarely prepared to extend their program to cover all situations. Few pacifists would insist that there be no laws regulating air and water pollution, driving speeds through congested areas, the sale and use of firearms, or the conduct of police or onlookers during a peaceful demonstration; or that such laws should not be enforced; or that enforcement must never involve coercive means, such as fines and imprisonment for law breakers.

Agreement by rational persuasion for some persons can mean coercion for others. In 1787, the American Constitutional Convention negotiated a peaceful settlement of the issues surrounding the new Constitution. One of the compromises of that convention was the perpetuation of slavery. A decade after slavery was abolished as a by-product of a fearfully destructive Civil War, peaceful compromises among national leaders in Washington permitted the rapid restoration of white supremacy in the South. An opponent of slavery or white supremacy confronted, then, the alternatives of persuading white southerners to abandon their beliefs and practices, a feat that even in retrospect seems impossible; to bring about change in the South by force or the threat of force; or to permit the South to impose a dreadful coercion on its black inhabitants.

If these examples show the difficulty in adhering consistently to a position stating that the use of intrinsically undesirable means of influence is never justifiable, they do not controvert the view that some of the means we believe we must employ are intrinsically bad. They help to show, rather, the tragic dilemma that political beings can face. One may or may not face this dilemma responsibly, but so far no one has discovered a way to avoid it.

A second response to this problem, then, is to hold that an action involving power and even coercion is sometimes better than any available alternative. Thus one may judge coercion to be intrinsically bad yet extrinsi-

cally or instrumentally desirable in some circumstances. This tension between the intrinsic undesirability of certain means of influence and their
unavoidability as instruments is one of the most poignant and troubling
problems in our lives as social and political beings.

A third response, following the logic of the second, is to see whether
it is possible to create a political system that would tend to reduce the use
of coercion and other undesirable forms of control, and tend to increase
the use of more desirable forms. To examine this possibility obviously requires us to consider some basic empirical questions. For example, are political systems really so much alike that the differences can hardly matter to
us all that much? Or, as I imagine most of us like to believe, do they differ
in some pretty important ways? If they do, how? To take one possibility,
how do democratic regimes differ from undemocratic regimes? And what
conditions in a country will tend to favor one kind of regime or the other?
Finally, to what extent is human nature a limit on various possibilities? To
what extent do people vary in the way they behave in political life? In the
next four chapters we shall briefly explore these questions.

As we have already seen, however, our interest in different forms of
control also reflects a concern for certain values or standards, which I have
barely touched on in the last few pages. For example, how, if at all, can we
justify a belief that a system based on agreement is better than one based
on coercion? Or that democracy is better than dictatorship? Or that people
have rights to "life, liberty, and the pursuit of happiness"? And so on. In
Chapter 10 we shall see how some recent writers have tried to come to grips
with issues like these.

FIVE
POLITICAL SYSTEMS:
SIMILARITIES

Just how many political systems are there in the world? No one knows. Given the broad definition of "political system" used here, they must number in the millions. In 1990 the globe was divided up into more than 170 nominally independent countries. Among these countries existed an increasingly dense network of political systems, including international organizations like the United Nations, regional organizations such as the European Community, and countless other associations and relationships, formal and informal, governmental and nongovernmental. Within each country were innumerable other political systems: territorial governmental units like states, counties, and municipalities; other governmental units like presidents, prime ministers, governors, mayors, legislatures, administrative organizations, and so on; systems not directly a part of the government of the state, such as business firms, labor unions, religious organizations, political parties, newspapers, educational institutions; and an infinite variety of other associations, from families to athletic leagues.

In the United States alone in 1987 there were 50 states, 3,042 counties, 19,205 municipal governments, 16,691 townships and towns, 14,741 school districts, and 29,487 other special districts. At about the same time there were 88 million households, 55 million families, 84,000 public elementary and secondary schools, 14,846 banks and 61,548 banking offices, 16 million corporations, partnerships, and proprietorships, and 2.1 million farms.[1]

Our systematic knowledge extends to only a small portion of the political behavior of a tiny number of these systems. Strange as it may seem, some highly important political systems have not usually been studied by political scientists (or for the most part by other social scientists) *as political systems* with relations of power and institutions for governing. Notable among these are the organizations within which people spend most of their daily lives: workplaces, business firms, economic enterprises. Nor have political scientists paid much attention to the diminutive political system within which people spend most of the rest of their daily lives—the family. What political scientists (and political philosophers) have focused on over many centuries is a small subset of political systems of truly extraordinary importance: those involved, more or less directly, in governing the state— the Government, as we called it in Chapter 1. Although in this chapter and the next our concern will be mainly with this crucial subset of political systems, it is important to keep in mind that in our daily lives we are enveloped in political systems—in relations of influence, control, power, and sometimes coercion—that we may not even perceive as having governments, despite the extent to which those governments press upon and shape our everyday existence.

The larger and more enduring systems studied by political scientists are essentially similar in some respects, and crucially different in others. It is to these similarities and differences that we now turn.

TWO EXTREME VIEWS

There are two extreme but common views about political systems. According to one, political systems never vary in their important aspects. According to the other, they are so plastic they can be molded to suit the heart's desire.

Even if, as is the case with practically all disagreements about politics, some of the differences in these perspectives are purely semantic, at base the conflict is more than a matter of words. Consider, for example, the hypothesis that all political systems are dominated by a ruling class or ruling elite, a view associated with three men whose lives spanned the tumultous changes in Europe during the last quarter of the nineteenth century and the first quarter of the twentieth. Two were eminent Italians: Vilfredo Par-

---

[1]U.S. Bureau of the Census, *Stastical Abstract of the United State: 1988,* 108th ed. (Washington, D.C.: U.S. Government Printing Office, 1987), Table 429, p. 256; Table 58, p. 44; Table 200, p. 124; Table 773, p. 471; Table 823, p. 495; and Table 1056, p. 608.

eto (1848–1923) and Gaetano Mosca (1858–1941); the third, who was of German birth, lived much of his life in Italy: Roberto Michels (1876–1936). All three achieved acclaim among social theorists disillusioned with or cynical about democracy. A statement by Mosca seems to catch the essence of their argument:

> Among the constant facts and tendencies that are to be found in all political organisms, one is so obvious that it is apparent to the most casual eye. In all societies—from societies that are very meagerly developed and have barely attained the dawnings of civilization, down to the most advanced and powerful societies—two classes of people appear—a class that rules and a class that is ruled. The first class, always the less numerous, performs all political functions, monopolizes power and enjoys the advantages that power brings, whereas the second, the more numerous class, is directed and controlled by the first, in a manner that is now more or less legal, now more less arbitrary and violent, and supplies the first, in appearance at least, with material means of subsistence and with the instrumentalities that are essential to the vitality of the political organism.[2]

At the opposite extreme are naive (but not always youthful) enthusiasts poised on the eve of Utopia's arrival, who proclaim, and may even believe, that when the New Day dawns "politics" will disappear.

Observers disagree about what is persistent in politics and what is open to change, and it would be misleading to suggest that in our present state of knowledge the matter can be firmly settled. Each of the extreme views incorporates some of the truth, but each is also incomplete.

As to the view that politics is infinitely plastic, a multitude of experience shows that after the sun rises on a new society "without politics," by high noon the "old" politics has returned with a vengeance. By some standards the new politics may be better, perhaps very much better, than the old; or it may be worse, perhaps very much worse; but in at least some respects the two will be very much alike.

[2]Mosca, *The Ruling Class* (*Elementi di Scienza Politica,* 1896), ed. Arthur Livingston (New York: McGraw-Hill Book, Co., 1939), p. 50. (Copyright 1939 by McGraw-Hill. Used by permission of McGraw-Hill Book Company.) The hypothesis is also set forth by Pareto in *The Mind and Society* (*Trattato di Sociologia Generale,* 1916), 4 vols. (New York: Harcourt Brace Jovanovich, 1935), in vol. 4, p. 1569, and by Michels, *Political Parties* (1915) (New York: Collier Books, 1962), p. 342 ff. A superb study of Mosca that includes as an appendix the final version of his theory of the ruling class is James H. Meisel, *The Myth of the Ruling Class* (Ann Arbor: University of Michigan Press, 1956). An excellent introduction to Pareto will be found in *Vilfredo Pareto: Sociological Writings,* selected and introduced by S. E. Finer (New York: Holt, Rinehart and Winston, 1966). See also S. E. Finer, "Pareto and Pluto-Democracy: The Retreat to Galapagos," *American Political Science Review,* 62 (June 1968), pp. 440–50. A succinct summary and critique of Michels is John D. May's "Democracy, Organization, Michels," *American Political Science Review,* 59 (June 1965), pp. 417–29.

It is these similarities, these stubborn and until now apparently inescapable regularities, to which I now wish to call your attention.

CHARACTERISTICS OF POLITICAL SYSTEMS

Uneven Control of Political Resources

Control over political resources is distributed unevenly. There are four reasons why this is so.

(1) Some specialization of function exists in every society; in advanced societies specialization is extensive. Specialization of function (the division of labor) creates differences in access to different political resources.

(2) Because of inherited differences, not all people start life with the same access to resources, and those with a head start often increase their lead. Individuals and societies are to some extent prisoners of the past; they never start with a completely clean slate either biologically or socially. Some endowments are biological. Many endowments, such as wealth, social standing, or the level of education and aspiration of one's parents, are not biological, however, but social. Whatever their source, differences in biological and social endowments at birth often multiply into even greater differences in resources among adults. Almost everywhere, for example, opportunities for education are related at least in part to the wealth, social standing, or political position of one's parents.

(3) Differences in biological and social inheritance, together with differences in experiences, all produce differences in the incentives and goals of different people in a society. Differences in motivation in turn lead to differences in skills and in resources: Not everyone is equally motivated to go into politics, to become a leader, or to acquire the resources that help the leader gain influence over others.

(4) Finally, some differences in incentives and goals usually are encouraged in societies in order to equip individuals for different specialities. The circle is complete: Whenever specialization of function is regarded as advantageous, some differences in motivations are also thought to be beneficial. But differences in motivations are likely to lead to differences in resources—for example, to greater military prowess for warriors than for shepherds.

For these four reasons[3] it appears to be impossible to create a society in which political resources would be distributed with perfect equality among adults. However, you must not conclude that there are no important

[3]For a comprehensive treatment, see Gerhard Lenski, *Power and Privilege* (New York: McGraw-Hill Book Co., 1966), especially Chap. Four.

differences in the way political resources are distributed in different societies. For there are differences, and they are important. That is a matter for the next chapter.

The Quest for Political Influence

Some members of the political system seek to gain influence over the policies, rules, and decisions enforced by the government—i.e., political influence. People seek political influence not necessarily for its own sake, but because control over the government helps them to achieve one or more of their goals. Control over the government is such a familiar way of furthering one's goals or values that it is hard to imagine a political system in which no one sought power.

Uneven Distribution of Political Influence

Political influence is distributed unevenly among the members of a political system. Clearly this proposition is closely related to the first one, which dealt with resources. Because some people have more resources with which they can influence the Government, it is easier for them to gain more influence over the Government if and when they wish to do so. People with more influence over the Government can use their influence to gain control over more political resources.

The existence of unequal political influence has been observed for centuries; yet although many observers agree on the fact, they disagree in appraising it, some of them justifying it and others attacking it. The opening book of Aristotle's *Politics* sought to explain and justify the differences in the authority of master and slave, husband and wife, parent and child. Twenty centuries later, in the midst of the Enlightenment, Rousseau sought to explain and to attack inequalities of power in his famous essay, *A Discourse on the Origins of Inequality* (1775). Rousseau traced the origins of inequalities of power to inequalities in property. Inequality in property, he maintained, led in turn to inequalities in other resources. Less than a century after Rousseau, Marx and Engels put forth a similar explanation in the *Communist Manifesto* and a series of revolutionary works that followed.

Sometimes the proposition that political influence is distributed unequally is confused with Mosca's hypothesis that in every political system there is a ruling class. But the one does not imply the other. We shall come back to this distinction in the next chapter, for the presence or absence of a ruling class is one respect in which political systems differ. It is true, though, that if we call the individuals with the greatest political influence the political leaders, then our third proposition implies that every political system has political leaders. And that is the sense in which we shall use the term "leader" or "political leader" in this book: to refer to those individuals who have the greatest influence in a political system.

The Pursuit and Resolution of Conflicting Aims

Members of a political system pursue conflicting aims, which are dealt with, among other means, by the government of the political system. Conflict and consensus are both important aspects of political systems. People who live together never agree about everything, but if they are to continue to live together, they cannot wholly disagree in their aims.

Although political theorists have recognized this duality, some have placed more stress on the one than the other. Some, like Hobbes, have emphasized the propensity of people to conflict with one another; others, like Aristotle and Rousseau, their propensity for agreement and cooperation.

The Government does not necessarily intervene every time the aims and acts of different individuals conflict. Conflict is often dealt with by nonpolitical means—by gossip, for example, or sorcery, or aggressive language, or even by isolated outbursts of violence.

In complex societies a good deal of conflict is mediated, arbitrated, suppressed, resolved, or handled in some fashion by political systems other than the State. However, when a degree of coercion is required that goes beyond what is possible or permitted to other governments operating in the territorial area of the State, officials of the Government can use their superior power by virtue of the Government's exclusive control over the conditions under which violence may be legitimately employed. Thus the Government steps in whenever the conflict is considered beyond adjustments by nonpolitical means or by governments other than that of the State.

The Acquisition of Legitimacy

Leaders in a political system try to ensure that whenever governmental means are used to deal with conflict, the decisions arrived at are widely accepted not solely from fear of violence, punishment, or coercion but also from a belief that it is morally right and proper to do so. According to one usage of the term, a government is said to be "legitimate" if the people to whom its orders are directed believe that the structure, procedures, acts, decisions, policies, officials, or leaders of government possess the quality of "rightness," propriety, or moral goodness—the right, in short, to make binding rules. Thus, our fourth proposition is equivalent to saying: Leaders in a political system try to endow their actions with legitimacy.

When a leader's influence is clothed with legitimacy, it usually is referred to as authority. Authority, then, is a special kind of influence, legitimate influence. Hence, our fourth proposition is also equivalent to: Leaders in a political system try to convert their influence into authority. Because they often succeed, legitimacy is widespread and important.

It is easy to see why leaders strive for legitimacy. Authority is a highly efficient form of influence. It is not only more reliable and durable than naked coercion but it also enables a ruler to govern with a minimum of political resources. It would be impossible to rely on fear and terror, for example, to carry out the complex tasks of a large bureaucratic organization such as the U.S. Postal Service, the Department of Defense, Massachusetts General Hospital, General Motors, or the public school system of New York City. Also it probably would be impossible, or at any rate much more costly, to rely simply on direct rewards, for this would require an unwieldy "piece-rate" system. When subordinates regard the orders and assignments they receive as morally binding, only a relatively small expenditure of resources, usually in the form of salaries and wages, is necessary to ensure satisfactory performance.

Although many different kinds of political systems can acquire legitimacy, democracies may be more in need of it than most other systems. In the long run, democracy cannot be forced on a group of people against their will; in fact, democracy is unlikely to survive when a large minority opposes it, for democratic institutions would encounter rough going if a majority always had to impose its rule on a large minority.

An enormous variety of political systems seem to have gained considerable legitimacy in various time and places. Even in the relatively democratic society of the United States, political systems that reflect quite contradictory principles of authority acquire legitimacy. For example, business firms, government agencies, and some religious associations are organized according to hierarchical rather than democratic principles. Yet many citizens who concede legitimacy to the American government because of its democratic structure also concede legitimacy to these hierarchical systems. In some time and place, almost every conceivable political arrangement—feudalism, monarchy, oligarchy, hereditary aristocracy, plutocracy, representative government, direct democracy—has acquired so much legitimacy that people have volunteered their lives in its defense.

Development of an Ideology

Leaders in a political system usually espouse a set of more or less persistent, integrated doctrines that purport to explain and justify their leadership in the system. A set of doctrines of this kind is often called a political ideology (Mosca called it a "political formula").[4] One reason why leaders develop an ideology is obvious: to endow their leadership with legitimacy, to convert their political influence into authority. And it is far more economical to rule by means of authority than by means of coercion.

[4]Mosca, *The Ruling Class*, pp. 70–71.

Some leaders, including the highest governmental officials and their allies, usually espouse an ideology that justifies not only their own leadership but also the political sysem itself. Their ideology is then the official or reigning ideology. A reigning ideology indicates the moral, religious, factual, and other assumptions that are assumed to justify the system. A highly developed reigning ideology usually contains standards for appraising the organization, policies, and leaders of the system, and also an idealized description of the way in which the system actually works, a version that narrows the gap between reality and the goal prescribed by the ideology.

Despite the fact that a reigning ideology helps incumbent leaders acquire legitimacy, it would be highly unrealistic to conclude that the existence or content of an ideology can be completely explained by the desires of leaders to clothe their actions with legitimacy and thus to transform naked power into authority. For one thing, the fact that many people who are not leaders accept the ideology reflects a desire for explanation, an interpretation of experiences and goals, that offers meaning and purpose to life and to one's place in the universe. It would be surprising if people who for thousands of years sought to comprehend the relative motions of planets and stars did not also want to understand their own political order. Moreover, despite appearances to the contrary, leaders cannot arbitrarily invent and manipulate a reigning ideology, for once a political ideology is widely accepted in a political system, the leaders, too, become its prisoners. They run the risk of undermining their own legitimacy if they violate its norms.

It would be unrealistic, however, to assume that a reigning ideology is a unified, consistent body of beliefs accepted by everyone in a political system. In the first place, the extent to which a distinguishable ideology is actually developed and articulated varies enormously from one political system to another. In the second place, no ideology is ever entirely integrated or internally consistent. For one thing, an ideology is not necessarily static: New situations create a need for new explanations and emphasis on new goals, and thus novel and unrelated or even inconsistent elements creep in. Then, too, a certain amount of ambiguity is sometimes a positive advantage precisely because it permits flexibility and change.

Third, a reigning ideology is probably never uniformly accepted by all members of a system. Many members have only rudimentary knowledge of the prevailing ideology articulated by the leaders; others may actually hold—perhaps unwittingly—a variety of private views that are at odds with the reigning ideology.

Fourth, the reigning ideology may be rejected. Some members of a political system—communists or fascists in a democratic country, or democrats in an authoritarian country—may adhere to rival and conflicting ideologies. Because people differ in their aims, incumbent leaders rarely rule without incurring opposition, overt or covert; few systems can count on ungrudging support from all their members. Opponents of a regime often formulate criticism that denies the existing system its legitimacy. Often, too, critics depict an alternative that, unlike their portrayal of the existing system, is held to repose on a legitimate foundation.

Sometimes the revolutionary ideology of one period becomes the reigning ideology of the next. In the eighteenth century, democratic doctrine was revolutionary ideology; today, it is the reigning ideology in the United States and most of western Europe. In Russia, Marxism and Leninism were revolutionary ideologies until 1917; they then became reigning ideologies modified by Lenin's successors. With the advent of Mikhail Gorbachev in 1986, they rapidly receded in the face of a new pragmatism.

The Impact of Other Political Systems

The way a political system behaves is influenced by the existence of other political systems. With occasional exceptions so rare that they can be ignored—a small and completely isolated club or tribe, for example—political systems do not exist in isolation.

Exceptional cases aside, every political system engages in foreign relations, for the actions open to one system are affected by the past or probable actions of others. A city cannot successfully ignore the existence of a national government; national governments must adapt their actions to the hard fact that other national governments, alliances, coalitions, and international organizations also exist. Even a club or a religious congregation cannot act with complete autonomy; and the leaders of a trade union must take into account the past or probable actions of business firms, other unions, and the government.

The influence of other political systems is so obvious that it would scarcely need mentioning if it were not for the curious fact that most people who portray their vision of an ideal political system ignore the limits imposed by the existence of other political systems. It is easy to imagine "the good society" if one does not bother with other, and quite possibly bad, societies that might clutter up the surrounding landscape. Consequently, political Utopias are usually portrayed without the troublesome limitations imposed by foreign relations, which are eliminated by either ignoring them entirely or solving them according to some simple plan.

The Inevitability of Change

It is appropriate to close this chapter by emphasizing a regularity that anticipates the subject of the next: *All political systems undergo change.*

From time immemorial political observers have pointed out the mutability of political systems. "Seeing that everything which has a beginning has also an end," wrote Plato, "even a constitution such as yours will not last forever, but will in time be dissolved." With his characteristic preference for imaginative and somewhat rigid theoretical notions drawn from brilliant speculation but not tested against concrete experience, Plato went on to describe the inevitable process of decay through which even the perfect aristocracy he proposed must degenerate into a "timocracy," or government of honor, to be followed by oligarchy, thence by democracy, and finally by tyranny.

Aristotle rejected Plato's dialectic, but he devoted a lengthy section of *The Politics* to the causes of revolutions and constitutional change; he extended the theory of political change well beyond where Plato had taken it. Because of their solid good sense, his remarks are still worth reading.

Although students of politics have observed the mutability of political systems, it is an interesting fact that those who set out to reveal the lineaments of an ideal State generally eliminate all change from their Utopia. Being perfect, the ideal State either cannot change or, if it changes at all, must change for the worse. Consequently, political Utopias exclude or deprecate the idea of change. Plato assumed that even his perfect State would change—but that it must inevitably decay into increasingly degenerate forms. (As Aristotle testily pointed out, "When it comese to tyrannies, Plato stops: He never explains whether they do, or do not, change, nor, if they do, why they do so, or into what constitution they change.") Karl Marx turned Plato around. Marx portrayed the whole of history as ceaseless and ineluctable change. Yet once the final state of communism was reached, all the historical forces that had hitherto made for change were, presumably, to vanish. Even democrats sometimes imply that democracy is a final state in humanity's political evolution. Yet in the entire history of political institutions, no political system has ever been immutable.

Because of the obvious and extraordinary importance of political change, whether peaceful or violent, evolutionary or revolutionary, many attempts have been made to understand it, explain it, and even predict it, to identify different types of change, the conditions that produce them, the sequences or stages through which changes proceed, and so on. Revolutions in particular have generated an enormous amount of investigation and theory. Yet we still lack a systematic understanding of political change or a satisfactory theory about revolution, and our capacity for predicting crucial political changes is still quite poor. Nonetheless, at least two predictions can be made with considerable confidence: (1) In every political system, no matter how solid it may be or appear to be, significant changes are bound to take place; and (2) because change is so difficult to predict, a very large measure of uncertainty is an inescapable feature of political life.

Perhaps in no other time has change been so marked a feature of political life—as indeed of all spheres of life—as it has been, throughout the world, in the century now drawing to a close. And there is every reason to believe that the pace and extent of change will be no less during the century to come.

SIX

POLITICAL SYSTEMS: DIFFERENCES

Schemes for classifying political systems into different types are, of course, as old as the study of politics itself. Aristotle, for example, produced a classification based on two criteria: the relative number of citizens entitled to rule, whether one, few, or many; and whether the rulers governed in "the common interest" or in their own selfish interests.[1] This famous sixfold classification (Table 6-1) has influenced thinking ever since. But a half century ago, Max Weber offered a classification that has had more influence among

TABLE 6-1   Aristotle's Classification

NO. CITIZENS ENTITLED TO RULE	RULERS RULE IN INTEREST OF	
	ALL.	THEMSELVES
One	Kingship (monarchy)	Tyranny
Few	Aristocracy	Oligarchy
Many	Polity	Democracy

[1]Ernest Barker, ed., *The Politics of Aristotle* (Oxford: Oxford University Press, 1952), Book 3, Chaps. Six and Eight, esp. pp. 110–14. Notice, however, that Aristotle later reveals a more complex scheme by equating oligarchy with rule by the rich and democracy with rule by the poor. See p. 116.

later social scientists than Aristotle's. Weber restricted his attention to systems in which the government was accepted as legitimate, and he suggested that the leaders of a political system might claim legitimacy for their rule, and members might accept their claims, on three grounds:

(1)   *Tradition:* Legitimacy rests "on an established belief in the sanctity of immemorial traditions" and on the need to obey leaders who exercise the authority according to the traditions. Weber held that this was "the most universal and primitive case" of authority.

(2)   *Exceptional Personal Qualities:* Legitimacy is based on "devotion to the specific and exceptional sanctity, heroism, or exemplary character of an individual person" and the moral or political order he or she has revealed or ordained.

(3)   *Legality:* Legitimacy rests on a belief that power is wielded in a way that is legal; the constitutional rules, the laws, and the powers of officials are accepted as binding because they are legal; what is done legally is regarded as legitimate.[2]

To each of these three main grounds for legitimacy, then, there corresponds a "pure" form of authority: (1) traditional authority, (2) charismatic authority (from a Greek word used by early Christians meaning "the gift of grace"), and (3) legal authority.

Weber recognized that these pure forms were abstractions or, as he called them, "ideal types." In an actual political system one might encounter all three kinds of legitimate authority.

Weber's and Aristotle's schemes have been all but pushed aside by the typologies that have crowded into political analysis in recent years.[3]

Is there one best typology? Obviously, no. There are thousands of criteria for classifying political systems. Which ones we find most useful will depend on the aspects of politics in which we are most interested. A geographer might distinguish political systems according to the area they occupy, a demographer by the number of persons who are members, a lawyer according to their legal codes. A philosopher or theologian interested in distinguishing "the best" political system will use ethical or religious criteria. A social scientist interested in determining how revolution is related to economic conditions might classify systems by relative income and frequency of revolutions. Just as there is no one best way of classifying people, so too there is no single way of distinguishing and classifying political systems superior to others for all purposes.

[2]Max Weber, *The Theory of Social and Economic Organization,* trans. A. M. Henderson and Talcott Parsons (New York: Oxford University Press, 1947), p. 328.

[3]Some of these, particularly those relevant to democratic systems, are summarized in Arend Lijphart, "Typologies of Democratic Systems," *Comparative Political Studies* 1 (April 1968), pp. 3–44. For his own typology, see his "Democratic Political Systems: Types, Cases, Causes, and Consequences," *Journal of Theoretical Politics* 1, no. 1 (January 1989), pp. 33–48.

If there are innumerable differences between political systems, some are associated with such a broad range of important consequences—particularly consequences for popular government—that they are particularly worth stressing. These are (1) paths to the present, (2) the socioecomomic "level" or degree of "modernity", (3) distribution of political resources and skills, (4) bases of cleavage and cohesion, (5) the magnitude or severity of conflicts, and (6) institutions for sharing and exercising power.

Although in some degree these differences apply to political systems of all sorts, let us focus the discussion by assuming as our frame of reference the political system of a country.

PATHS TO THE PRESENT

Every political system has had, in some respects, a unique past. This is more than an abstract point, for the inheritance of the past bears heavily on the present and influences the future. Differences in their past mean that the countries of the world do not have exactly the same options. A people that has known nothing but centuries of authoritarian rule is not likely to turn into a stable democracy in a week. And as we shall see in a moment, a country's particular path to the present often makes an all but ineradicable imprint on its conflicts, so powerful that internal peace and stability cannot possibly be brought about by a few months of negotiations.

DEGREE OF "MODERNITY"

History leaves political systems embedded in societies that are at different stages of "development" or "modernization." These terms, now widely used among political scientists, have a parochial air about them, but their meaning can be make quite specific—enough so, indeed, to allow for measurement. There are, in short, profound differences from one country to another in the amount of income per capita, literacy, education, technical skills, technology, industrialization, urbanization, newspaper and magazine circulation, electronic communications, transportation facilities, and the like. These all tend to be intercorrelated: A country relatively low (less "developed") in one respect will very likely be relatively low in other respects, and the converse is true as well.[4]

In Table 6–2, 149 countries are divided into five categories according to GNP per capita. As the table shows, the higher a country's per capita

[4]See Tatu Vanhanen, *The Emergence of Democracy, A Comparative Study of 119 States, 1850–1979* (Helsinki: The Finnish Society of Arts and Letters, 1984), Tables 3 and 4, pp. 46–47; Bruce M. Russett et al., *World Handbook of Political and Social Indicators* (New Haven, Conn.: Yale University Press, 1964).

TABLE 6-2   Countries by GNP and Other Characteristics

FIFTH	N	GNP PER CAP	PERCENT SCHOOL AGE POPULATION IN SCHOOL	LITERACY RATE	POPULATION PER PHYSICIAN	INFANT MORTALITY RATE
1st	30	12128	64	88	645	23
2nd	30	3224	63	87	1392	37
3rd	30	1149	55	68	5731	69
4th	30	500	46	48	9001	107
5th	29	235	35	39	24077	121

Sources: GNP per capita from The World Bank, *World Tables,* 3d ed., (Baltimore: Johns Hopkins University Press, 1983), vol. 1, *Comparative Economic Data,* Table II, pp. 560–565 and Table IV, pp. 510–15. For the Soviet Union and Eastern Europe and several other countries not in the World Bank data, GNP per capita is from U.S. Bureau of the Census, *Statistical Abstract of the United States 1988,* 108th ed. (Washington: U.S. Government Printing Office, 1987), Table 1387, p. 805. Other characteristics from Ruth Leger Sivard, *World Military and Social Expenditures,* 11th ed. (Washington, D.C.: World Priorties, 1986), Table II, pp. 33–46 and Table III, pp. 36–41.

GNP, the greater the percentage of the school-age population enrolled in school, the higher the literacy rate, the smaller the number of persons per physician, and the lower the infant mortality rate.[5] One could find similar relations with many other variables of the kind mentioned in the previous paragraph. Thus GNP per capita is a useful indicator—but not because of what it signifies standing by itself. We shall see in the next chapter that several of the countries with the highest GNP per capita are ranked much lower on the other factors in Table 6–2. As the table suggests, however, for most countries GNP per capita is closely associated with many other important features of the country's society. Generally speaking, the societies of the countries in the top fifth of the table are radically different from those in third, fourth, or lowest categories. It so happens that the societies of countries in the top fifth possess a variety of features particularly favorable to democratic regimes. By contrast, the lower a country stands in the table, the less favorable are the conditions for democracy. We shall return to this important point in the next chapter.

DISTRIBUTION OF POLITICAL RESOURCES AND SKILLS

Political resources and skills are distributed in different ways in different political systems. Although they are distributed unequally in all systems, the degree of inequality varies from one system to the next. For example,

[5]It is worth bearing in mind that data on GNP and other indicators should be treated with some caution. Cross-national comparisons of GNP are risky. Moreover, the bureaucratic capacities for collecting statistics vary greatly. Scholars have reported incidents in some less

knowledge is a political resource that contributes to the formation of political skills. Access to knowledge through literacy and education is distributed unequally; but in some countries the inequality is greater than in others. In a considerable number of countries, more than half the people over 15 are unable to read and write, while in others virtually every person over 15 can do so (Table 6-3). In some countries eight out of every ten persons between the ages of 5 and 19 attend school; in others fewer than three out of ten do so (Table 6-4). The variation in the proportions who attend institutions of higher education is even more extreme.[6]

Wealth is a political resource, and wealth is distributed unequally everywhere, but the degree of inequality varies. For example, the distribution of land, an important form of wealth in agricultural countries, is markedly unequal in all countries. But the inequality in landholdings was considerably more extreme in Iraq, where half the total acreage was occupied by 0.7 percent of the farms, than in Denmark, where half the acreage was taken up by 21 percent of the farms. (See Figure 6-1).

The extent to which inequalities are correlated also varies from society to society. Suppose every person in a political system were ranked according to relative standing with respect to the most important political resources in that society: let us say wealth, income, knowledge, popularity, control over communications, and command over police and military forces. If everyone's relative standing were the same, thus resulting in a perfect correlation, inequalities in resources would be completely cumulative. The more

TABLE 6-3   Literacy Rates of 137 Countries

LITERACY RATE* (%)	NUMBER OF COUNTRIES
100	2
90–99	22
80–89	20
70–79	28
60–69	13
50–59	13
under 50%	39
N:	137

*Among persons over 15.

Source: Sivard, *World Military and Social Expenditures,* Table 3, pp. 36ff.

developed countries of data that were obviously made up by officials. The error in infant mortality rates is probably very high.

[6]See Charles Lewis Taylor and Michael C. Hudson, *World Handbook of Political and Social Indicators* (New Haven, Conn.: Yale University Press, 1972), Tables 4.4 and 5.5.

**TABLE 6-4   Percentage of School-Age
Children (Ages 5–19) in School**

PERCENTAGE	NUMBER OF COUNTRIES
80	6
70–79	15
60–69	38
50–59	29
40–49	19
30–39	12
20–29	9
under 20%	7
N:	135

Source: Sivard, *World Military and Social Expenditures,* Table 3, pp. 36ff.

of one resource an individual had, the more that individual would have
of the rest. If, however, an individual's standing on one ranking bore no
relationship to other rankings (there is no correlation), inequalities in resources would be dispersed. Dispersion does not mean equality: In a system
with completely dispersed inequalities, there could be inequality with respect to every political resource. Nonetheless, the difference between cumu-

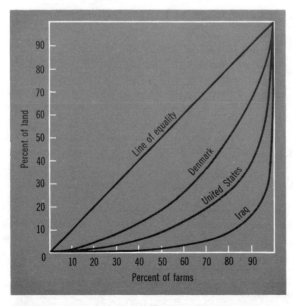

FIGURE 6-1 Lorenz Curve of Land Distribution Source: Taylor and Hudson, *World Handbook,* Table
4.14, pp. 267–68.

lative and dispersed inequalities is a crucial one, for in a society of dispersed inequalities, people lacking one resource might make up for it by having greater control over other resources.

Neither type exists in pure form. There is a strong tendency toward cumulative inequality, yet there appear to be significant differences in the inequalities among political systems. In countries still remaining at one of the three lower levels in Table 6-2, inequalities are usually highly cumulative. In societies undergoing an industrial revolution, however, wealth and income shift away from an older feudal aristrocracy or landed oligarchy toward the new leaders—in industry, banking, and commerce. Yet for the bulk of the population, in spite of rising incomes, inequalities are still strongly cumulative. (This is the stage that Marx witnessed in western Europe in the mid–nineteenth century.) Following a period of industrialization, some countries have made a further transition to a new kind of society—modern, dynamic, pluralistic. As incomes and mass consumption continue to increase, there is a further diffusion of technology, literacy, education, affluence, and mass communication. This diffusion also may be accompanied by a marked expansion in interest-group organizations, political skills, and the suffrage. Even in these circumstances inequalities in political resources still persist, but they become less cumulative and more dispersed. Hence it becomes difficult to identify a small, well-defined elite that "runs the country," for different elites tend to exercise influence over different scopes of activity and their relations become highly complex. For example, information and knowledge become unusually important resources for gaining and maintaining influence, and varic⹁s "information and knowledge elites" come to play crucial roles in decisions. The influence of a president's national security advisor, a Senator's administrative assistant, the staff of a congressional committee, and the director of Central Intelligence requires skill in receiving, interpreting, shaping, and transmitting crucial, important information often highly specialized and technical, to other key decision makers. But it is not only at these high levels that the need for information enables specialists to acquire influence on decisions; more and more, decision makers within all the institutions of a modern society depend on them, whether local governments, firms in industry, commerce, and finance, trade unions, political parties, or international organizations.

CLEAVAGE AND COHESION

The patterns of political disagreement, conflict, and coalition have different causes in different systems. This proposition and the following paragraphs should be read with caution: It opposes a widespread view that political conflict can be explained by a single source of cleavage, usually an economic characteristic like "class" or "property."

In spite of an enormous amount of speculation, theory, and research, our understanding of political conflict is still limited. Single-factor explanations simply do not stand up well against the data now available. The kinds of individual and group characteristics that are associated with political conflict in countries include not only differences in social status, economic class, income, wealth, and occupation, but also in education, ideology, religion, language, region, and family origins. This multiplicity of factors creates different patterns of political cleavage and cohesion from one country to another.

In the first place, history has left countries with different legacies of characteristics that foster cleavages and cohesiveness, such as language. Because of our experience, Americans may be accustomed to believing that other countries have only one language, which many do; yet our neighbor, Canada, has two. Or compare the Low Countries: The Netherlands has a single language, yet in neighboring Belgium a linguistic boundary has existed for over a thousand years that runs across modern Belgium and divides Walloons, who speak French, from Flemings who speak Flemish, a Germanic language. In Switzerland the boundary between the French- and German-speaking zones has barely changed since it first evolved in the fifth century A.D. On the other side of the world the Indians have over 15 major languages and 500 minor languages and dialects. In fact, in India many minority languages—English is one—are spoken by more people than there are in all of Sweden.[7]

In the second place, history has left varying memories of the past treatment of these differences. Take racial differences. In the United States the enslavement of people of African origin created a castelike system of discrimination that survived long after the abolition of slavery, continues with diminishing force to the present day, and has been the soure of severe conflict. By contrast, in Brazil, where an even higher proportion of the population were of African origin and where slavery was not fully abolished until a generation after the American Civil War, the dominant population, which was mainly of Portuguese origin, accepted racial intermixing much more readily. Because of this, even though racial discrimination exists in Brazil, it has not been a major source of conflict, unlike in the United States. Or consider language again. The Swiss nation was built upon equality among

---

[7]Something of the range of variation in the historical legacy of differences will be found in Marie R. Haug, "Social and Cultural Pluralism as a Concept in Social System Analysis," *American Journal of Sociology* 73 (November 1967), pp. 294–304. The author classifies 114 countries according to an Index of Pluralism to reflect the amount of heterogeneity in language, race, religion, sectionalism, and ethnic groups. See also Table 4.15, "Ethnic and Linguistic Fractionalization" (in 136 countries) in Charles Lewis Taylor and Michael C. Hudson, *World Handbook of Political and Social Indicators* (New Haven, Conn.: Yale University Press, 1971), pp. 271–74.

its languages; as a result, political conflicts and resentments caused by linguistic differences are nearly negligible. In Belgium, on the other hand, after a flourishing period of Flemish prosperity and preeminence (its brilliance is reflected in the great Flemish painters of the time), an economic and cultural decline led to the subordination of the Flemish to the Walloons, a condition that embittered Belgian politics. In recent years, the economic decline of the Flemish areas has been reversed, while the Walloon region has declined, leading to resentment among the Walloons. Or take religion. In the United States, controversy between religious groups has been comparatively mild. But the conflict between the Protestant majority and Catholic minority in Northern Ireland leads to daily violence and frequent killing. In the Middle East, an almost impenetrable tangle of conflicts involve Moslems, Jews, and Christians, Israelis and Arabs, Moslem Arabs in Iraq and Moslem (but non-Arab) Iranians, Sunni Moslems and Shiite Moslems.

Finally, different stages of development tend to generate different forces stimulating cleavages and coalitions. In the nineteenth century, urbanization and industrialization in western European countries were accompanied by the misery and conflict that Marx was confident would finally polarize into a clear-cut conflict between an expanding urban proletariat and a decreasing capitalist bourgeoisie in which the proletariat was bound to win. Yet from the perspective of a later century, it appears that Marx was too hasty in extrapolating the early phases of industrialization into the indefinite future. Marx witnessed western Europe during the Industrial Revolution. He accurately foresaw that political conflicts would take place over demands for transforming the circumstances of the urban working classes. What he did not foresee was that long before the "bourgeoisie" was defeated in a conflict with the proletariat, three things would happen: The Industrial Revolution would begin to be transformed into a stage of high mass consumption; the industrial proletariat would shrink in size and become an increasingly smaller minority of the total working force;[8] and because many demands put forward by leaders of the working classes would be met, the industrial proletariat, a minority, would become increasingly unresponsive to militant appeals for revolutionary change.

Yet in countries now passing through an industrial revolution, conflicts over demands for ameliorating or transforming the situation of urban workers are likely to be a prominent feature of political life. Meanwhile, new social and ideological bases of conflict are emerging in the high mass consumption societies.

---

[8]It does not follow, however, that the working classes have become a minority. For a presentation of statistics to the contrary, see Andrew Levison, *The Working Class Majority* (New York: Coward, McCann & Geoghegan, 1974).

THE SEVERITY OF CONFLICT

The severity of conflict varies over time within any given system and from one system to another during the same period of time. Whatever difficulties may lurk in this proposition must not be allowed to obscure the fact that on common-sense grounds the proposition is hardly open to doubt. More than a century ago, Americans were engaged in killing one another on a massive scale in a civil war: That obviously was a severe conflict. The coup in Indonesia in 1966 in which the Sukarno regime was overturned and several hundred thousand people were killed was unquestionably a severe conflict. Armed rebellion, civil war, violent revolution, guerilla warfare, street battles, mass exile: These are conflicts of extreme severity. Speeches, debates, peaceful assembly, and peaceful elections are not.

Within any particular country, the temperature of political conflict fluctuates. Even the most stable countries are likely to have had a time of great turbulence and violence, a time of uprising, regicide, internal war— a "time of troubles." But the temperature of politics also fluctuates over short time periods. The Civil War marks the period of our most extreme conflict, but there has also been a conflict of considerable severity about once a generation throughout our national history, beginning with the Alien and Sedition laws at the end of the first decade under our Constitution.

During any particular period of time, however, some countries are more peaceful than others in their internal politics. While some countries may be passing through their historic Time of Troubles, others are basking in a mood of reconciliation and unity. It is even plausible that national differences in culture and temperament may make people in some countries more prone than those in others to seek peaceful, consensual solutions to their disputes. However that may be, it is clear that in any particular decade, conflict is more severe in some countries than in others.

Naturally, it is not easy to design satisfactory measurements for a concept such as "severity of conflict," nor to gather and interpret the data. More than a half century ago, a pioneering effort of this kind was carried out by a sociologist, Pitirum A. Sorokin. Despite the high level of his work, his findings have been largely neglected. Sorokin applied intelligently designed indicators of "disturbances" in French history from A.D. 526 to 1925, as well as to Ancient Greece, Ancient Rome, Byzantium, Germany and Austria, England, Italy, Spain, the Netherlands, Russia, Poland, and Europe as a whole. From his enormous and painstaking studies, Sorokin concluded:

> On the average in most countries studied, for every year with a significant social disturbance there have been only five years free from disturbances.
>
> It is not true that some nations are more orderly than others: all nations are orderly and disorderly, according to the time.

While there are some differences among nations with respect to the violence and intensity of disturbances, these differences are neither great nor consistent.

Only about 5 percent of all the disturbances on record occurred without violence; about a fourth occurred with slight violence, however. The possibilities of a "bloodless revolution," it seems, are slight.

Most disturbances last only a few weeks.

The indicators show no continuous trend either toward bigger and better "orderly progress" or toward ever-increasing disorderliness.

There is no association between internal disturbances and international war.

Disturbances occur not only in periods of decay and decline of society but in periods of blossoming and healthy growth.

What is crucial is the sociocultural network of values and relations: When the network is integrated and strong, disturbances are at a minimum.[9]

More recently, other social scientists have returned to this important topic. In 1969, in a report to the United States National Commission on the Causes and Prevention of Violence, a political scientist compared the amount of conflict in 114 countries. He found that between 1961 and 1965

TABLE 6-5   Civil Strife in the United States During the Turbulent Sixties, Compared with Other Nations

	UNITED STATES	17 DEMOCRATIC EUROPEAN NATIONS	113 COUNTRIES
Pervasiveness: No. participants			
per 100,000 population	1,116	676	683
Rank of the U.S.		7th	27th
Intensity: Casualties from strife			
per 10 million population	477	121	20,100
Rank of the U.S.		3rd	53rd
Duration: Rank of the U.S.		1st	6th
Total Magnitude of Civil Strife:			
Rank of the U.S.		1st	24th
Rank of the U.S., 1961–1965		5th	41st

The figures for the United States are for 1963–68; for other countries, 1961–65.

Source: Ted Robert Gurr, "A Comparative Study of Civil Strife," in Hugh Davis Graham and Ted Robert Gurr, *The History of Violence in America; A Report to the National Commission on the Causes and Prevention of Violence* (New York: Bantam Books, 1969), pp. 572–632, Table 17–2, p. 578, and Table 17–15, p. 628.

[9]Pitirim A. Sorokin, *Social and Cultural Dynamics,* vol. 3 (Boston: D.C. Heath & Co., 1937), Chap. Fourteen.

the magnitude of civil strife varied from ravaging civil wars and extensive mass violence in countries like the Congo, Indonesia, and South Vietnam to a total absence of any record of civil conflict in such countries as Sweden, Romania, Norway, and Taiwan.[10] Comparisons with the United States during its exceptionally turbulent years from 1963 to 1968 are shown in Table 6–5.

INSTITUTIONS FOR SHARING AND EXERCISING POWER

Finally, *political systems differ in their institutions for sharing and exercising power.* Many of us believe a corollary: that *political systems also differ in the distribution of power*—in the extent to which, in Aristotle's terms, power is distributed to one, few, or many. But given the problems in observing and measuring power discussed in Chapter 3, belief in this corollary must rest almost entirely on indirect evidence. And the most persuasive indirect evidence is the difference in the institutions that provide opportunities for citizens to share in the process of making policies enforced by the Government. These differences are the subject of the next chapter.

---

[10]Ted Robert Gurr, "A Comparative Study of Civil Strife," in Hugh Davis Graham and Ted Robert Gurr, *The History of Violence in America: A Report to the National Commission on the Causes and Prevention of Violence* (New York: Bantam Books, Inc., 1969), pp. 572–632. See also Ivo K. Feierabend, Rosalind L. Feierabend, and Betty A. Nesvold, "Social Change and Political Violence: Cross-National Patterns," pp. 632–87 of the same volume.

SEVEN

DIFFERENCES: POLYARCHIES AND NONPOLYARCHIES

Among the differences in political systems that make a difference—indeed a crucial difference—are their institutions for sharing and exercising power[1]. Popular governments provide far greater opportunities than other political systems for people to participate in making the laws they must obey. In ancient Greece, where popular government first appeared around 500 B.C., these systems were called democracies. At about the same time, popular government also arose among the Romans, who called their system a republic. For the moment, I shall simply call such systems popular governments.

For the next two thousand years the ideas and practices of popular government were shaped by the experiences of Greece—mainly in the city of Athens—and Rome. Even after the practice of popular government was superseded in Greece and Rome by hegemonic regimes, ideas about popular government continued to be dominated by Greek and Roman experience. Central to that experience was a belief in the desirability of govern-

---

[1] For a more extended treatment of the matter of this chapter, see my *Democracy and Its Critics* (New Haven, Conn.: Yale University Press, 1989), particularly Chapters 16 and 17.

ment by means of assemblies that all citizens were entitled to attend.[2] For this and other reasons, the prevailing assumption for almost two millenia was that popular government was necessarily restricted to small systems like city-states.

POLYARCHY

In the seventeenth and eighteenth centuries, this assumption was challenged by a new breed of advocates of popular government, who contended that *representation* was a feasible and desirable alternative to direct participation in a citizen assembly. What began to develop in both theory and practice was a wholly new form of popular government, radically different in many important respects from all systems that had hitherto existed for governing states, including Greek democracies, the Roman republic, and the city-state republics of medieval and Rennaissance Italy. Variously called republics, democracies, representative governments, democratic republics, or parliamentary systems,[3] these novel political systems extended the theory and practice of popular government far beyond the narrow boundaries of the city-state to the much larger domain of the country or national state.

THE POLITICAL INSTITUTIONS OF POLYARCHY

What made these systems historically new was their unique combination of political institutions. Of these, seven, to be discussed below, are of singular importance. Although some of these institutions developed in rudimentary fashion in a few countries during the nineteenth century, they did not attain their present form until the twentieth century. In this century the institu-

---

[2]As the Roman Republic expanded beyond the original city to all of Italy and beyond and conferred citizenship to its subjects, the assemblies held in Rome were attended by an increasingly smaller proportion of the citizen body, consisting of those who lived near Rome or had the wealth, time, and incentive to make the journey. Thus direct citizen participation in lawmaking became a mockery of the original idea and practice. Even so, the Romans never adopted a representative government as an alternative.

[3]It is sometimes argued that in the eighteenth century, "democracy" meant direct or assembly government, while "republic" referred to representative government. The authority often cited is James Madison, who in a renowned essay in defense of the proposed new constitution for the United States made such a distinction between "pure democracy" and a republic. Alexander Hamilton, John Jay, and James Madison, *The Federalist* (New York: The Modern Library, n.d.), pp. 58–59. However, an examination of eighteenth-century political rhetoric in America has demonstrated that the two terms were used interchangeably, often by the same speaker in the same sentence. Cf. Willi Paul Adams, *The First American Constitutions, Republican Ideology and the Making of State Constitutions in the Revoutionary Era*, trans. Rita and Robert Kimber (Chapel Hill, N.C.: The University of North Carolina Press, 1980), Chap. 4, "'Republic' and 'Democracy' in Political Rhetoric," pp. 99–117.

tions that, taken together, distinguish modern popular government from all earlier popular systems and from all other regimes, contemporary or historical, have come to be these:

1. Control over government decisions about policy is constitutionally vested in elected officials.

Among some of the oldest and sturdiest democratic countries of the present day, this crucial institution is a creation of the late nineteenth or early twentieth century. In France, for example, it was not firmly in place until the advent of the Third Republic in 1871. Making the prime minister and cabinet depend on a majority of votes in parliament rather than appointment by the monarch arrived even later in the Scandinavian countries: in Norway in 1884, in Denmark in 1915, and in Sweden in 1918.

2. Elected officials are chosen and peacefully removed in frequent, fair, and free elections in which coercion is absent or quite limited.

Like accountability, the secret ballot, which is now widely assumed to be required for fair and free elections, was a fairly late arrival in popular governments, rarely being regularly employed in national elections until the 1880s and in many countries not until the early years of this century.

3. Virtually all adults have the right to vote.
4. Most adults also have the right to run for public offices in these elections.

These two institutions reflect a profound change in the way we have come to think about democracy in theory and in practice. Until the present century, all democracies and republics had excluded a very large proportion of adults from participating in making the laws to which they were subject. In the renowned democracy of Athens, women were excluded, few foreigners were ever able to acquire citizenship even after generations of living in the city and contributing to its finances and its glories, and slaves, a sizeable part of the population, were excluded. Until the twentieth century half of all adults—women—were denied the right to vote in national elections in every country, including countries like Switzerland and the United States, which were among the oldest "democracies" in the world.[4] In the United States, despite the explicit words of the Fifteenth Amendment prohibiting

---

[4]In the countries where the political institutions listed here have existed continuously since 1950, women typically gained the suffrage between 1910 and 1930. In the United States women gained the right to vote in federal elections in 1920 following the passage of the Nineteenth Amendment. In France and Belgium women were excluded until World War II, and in Switzerland they did not have a constitutional right to vote in federal elections until 1971.

discrimination in the suffrage based on race,[5] throughout most of the old South blacks were effectively prevented from voting until after the passage and enforcement of federal civil rights acts in the 1960s.

5. Citizens possess a right, effectively enforced by judicial and administrative officials, to freedom of expression, including criticism of and opposition to the leaders or party in office.
6. They have access, and an effectively enforced right to gain access, to sources of information that are not monopolized by the government of the state, or by any other single group.
7. They possess an effectively enforced right to form and join political organizations, including political parties and interest groups.

When we speak today of "democracy" or "a democratic country" we generally mean a country in which these seven institutions exist. However, the term democracy is also commonly used in its nineteenth-century sense, when it referred to countries in which all of the institutions existed except for the third and fourth—that is, a universal or nearly universal inclusion of adults as full citizens. As we just saw, universal inclusion is essentially a twentieth-century development. When the famous two volumes, *Democracy in America,* by the great French writer Alexis de Tocqueville were published in 1835 and 1840, no one in America or Europe questioned the appropriateness of the title, despite the fact that only a minority of adults—white males—were full citizens who possessed the right to vote and to engage in public affairs.

Was the United States a democracy in the nineteenth century, despite its restrictionson full citizenship? *Is* it a democracy today? Because of the ambiguity and multiple meanings of the term democracy, I find it useful to call a political system in which the seven institutions are present a *polyarchy* or a *democratic polyarchy,* though I want to follow ordinary practice by referring to a country governed by polyarchy as a democratic country.

Systems in which one or more of the seven institutions are absent, or exist distinctly below the threshold of polyarchy, constitute a large, important, and highly diverse category of historical and contemporary systems. The nonpolyarchies of the contemporary world are often referred to as authoritarian, hegemonic, totalitarian, or dictatorial regimes. Unfortunately, any single term suggests too simple a picture of the complex diversity of political systems in the modern world, as we shall see. Despite this, for convenience I am going to lump them all together and call them nonpolyarchies or authoritarian regimes.

---

[5]Passed in 1870 in the wake of the Civil War, the amendment reads: "The right of citizens of the United States to vote shall not be denied or abridged by the United States or any State on account of race, color, or previous condition of servitude."

The Growth of Polyarchy

Because of the restrictions on suffrage noted earlier, no full polyarchies existed until this century. However, during the latter half of the nineteenth century all the institutions other than a fully inclusive citizen body did develop in some countries. Since 1850, the number of polyarchies (male or full) has increased more or less steadily, except for two periods of decline, one between 1920 and 1940, the other in the 1960s (Figure 7-1).[6] Yet because the number of countries in the world has also increased, in 1990 polyarchies constituted about the same proportion of the total as they had a half century or so earlier (Figure 7-2).

Further Differences Between Polyarchies and Nonpolyarchies

It is not only the seven political institutions just described that distinguish polyarchies fron nonpolyarchies. Countries in which the government of the state is a democratic polyarchy also differ in certain other important respects from countries governed by nonpolyarchal regimes.

Political Rights. One rather obvious difference is the existence in polyarchies of an extensive network of fundamental political rights. Many of these are simply an integral part of one or more of the seven institutions of polyarchy. Rights, effectively enforced by judicial and administrative, are necessary to the existence and functioning of the institutions: rights to vote in free and fair elections, to oppose officials and their policies, to organize political parties, interest groups, and other associations, and so on. In addition, however, people in countries that sustain polyarchal institutions over an extended period of time are likely also to share political attitudes and beliefs that support many other rights and freedoms as well. Thus the network of rights tends to extend well beyond those strictly necessary for the functioning of the institutions of polyarchy.

Pluralism: Autonomy vs. Control. Individuals and subsystems are more autonomous in relation to the Government of the State in polyarchies than in nonpolyarchies. To be sure, the difference is partly true by definition. In effect, what we mean by a polyarchy is a system with, among other things, a relatively higher tolerance for individual and organizational auton-

---

[6]It should be noted that in Figures 7-1 and 7-2, a country is counted as a male or restricted suffrage polyarchy prior to universal male suffrage if at least 10 percent of the total population actually voted in national elections. This is one of the two thresholds for the emergence of democracy used by Tatu Vanhanen in *The Emergence of Democracy: A Comparative Study of 119 States, 1850–1979* (Helsinki: The Finnish Society of Sciences and Letters, 1984). Vanhanen's other threshold is crossed "when the share of the smaller parties is at least 30 percent" (p. 33).

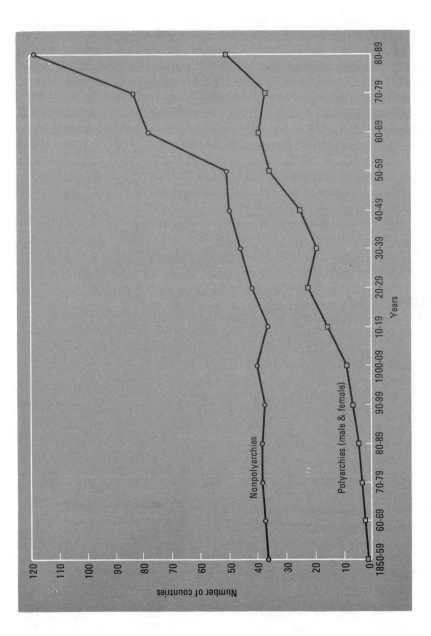

FIGURE 7-1. The growth of polyarchy, 1850–1990. Sources: Tatu Vanhanen, *The Emergence of Democracy: A Comparative Study of 119 States* (Helsinki: The Finnish Society of Arts and letters, 1984); Michael Coppedge and Wolfgange Reinicke, "A Measure of Polyarchy," paper prepared for the Conference on Measuring Democracy, Hoover Institution, Stanford University, May 27–28, 1988. The table also contains additional data from unpublished research by Coppedge, Reinicke, and Dahl.

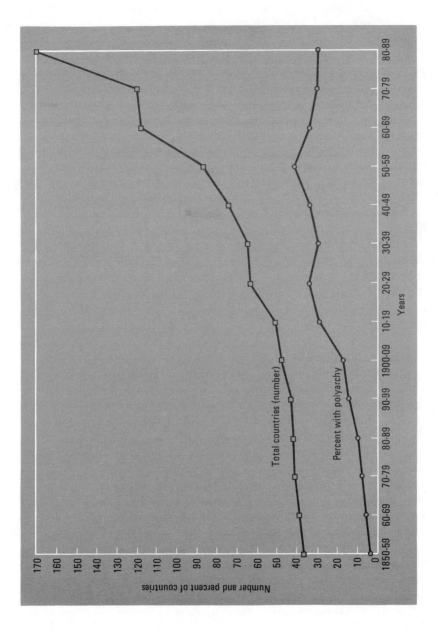

FIGURE 7-2. Countries with Polyarchy as Percent of All Countries, 1850–1990. Sources: See Figure 7–1.

omy. The rights to participate in and to oppose the government, the hall-mark of polyarchy, require the state to tolerate and even protect autonomy both for individuals and for organizations.

As a consequence of these rights, organizations of untold variety tend to exist in polyarchies: private clubs, cultural organizations, pressure groups, political parties, trade unions, and so on. Many of these organizations actively seek to influence the government; many more can be mobilized when their members believe that crucial interests are threatened. Political systems in which numerous relatively autonomous groups and organizations exist are often said to be *pluralist*.

By contrast, the development of autonomy threatens the nature of an authoritarian regime and the power of its leaders. Autonomous *organizations* are particularly dangerous. Hence organizations must be kept under the control of the government. Thus by comparison with the pluralism of poly-archies, authoritarian systems are more *monistic*. In the most extreme cases, authoritarian rulers have attempted to ensure that every individual and every organization is part of an all–embracing system of hierarchical con-trols. Although this limit is never reached in practice, it has sometimes been closely approached—for example, in the Soviety Union during the later period of Stalin's rule and in Germany under Hitler. It was for this reason that, as we saw earlier, a new name—totalitarian—was invented for these regimes.

Persuasion vs. Coercion.   In polyarchies, as opposed to nonpolyar-chies, political leaders rely more on persuasion and less on coercion.[7] Some forms of coercion are by definition excluded or minimized in polyarchies. A regime that imprisons the leaders of opposition parties or suppresses critical newspapers, for example, is by definition not a polyarchy. Con-versely, by definition a polyarchy must provide its people with rights to participate in choosing and opposing political leaders. An inclusive polyar-chy extends these rights to almost all the adult population.

That these differences distinguish polyarchies from nonpolyarchies merely by definition does not make them less significant, since they reflect actual differences among real systems. Moreover, the difference in the bal-ance of persuasion versus coercion is a practical consequence of the differ-ences in the political institutions themselves. A group that has an effective right to participate in the choice of political leaders is less likely to be co-erced in a conflict than a group without this right. This is most obvious if the group is numerous enough to consitute a majority. As long as the institu-tions of popular government are unimpaired, any attempt to coerce a ma-

---

[7]Although he uses a different typology of political systems, David Apter presents a simi-lar argument in *Choice and the Politics of Allocation* (New Haven, Conn.: Yale University Press, 1971), pp. 32–33, and passim.

jority of the population would be certain to fail, since a coerced majority could simply vote against the incumbents at the next election and replace them with more responsive officials. Because of this situation, politicians in polyarchies are rarely so foolhardy as to support laws directed against a majority of the people; if they ignore popular opinion, it is likely to cost them dearly. Of course, since laws rarely enjoy unanimous support, in any regime some persons could be coerced by laws that deprived them of some previous opportunity, privilege, or right. But even if people who participate in decisions sometimes suffer from the outcome, those who cannot partici- pate at all are even more likely to suffer. It seems improbable that the Con- stitutional Convention would have permitted slavery in America if the black people in this country had possessed the same rights to political participa- tion that white Americans had. In order to impose white supremacy on the recently liberated slaves after the Civil War, southern blacks were deprived of their newly acquired right to participate in politics.

In a polyarchy, it is usually difficult to coerce a large number of people, even if not a majority. For while extensive coercion places a strain on any political system, popular governments find it the most difficult. If civil disobedience on a grand scale, or even civil war, is to be avoided, a government engaged in coercing large minorities needs to have an impos- ing array of coercive forces at its disposal—a centralized and disciplined police system, a secret police, a compliant judiciary, military, and bureau- cratic establishments ready to obey the government when "duty" requires the coercion of large numbers of fellow citizens, and a body of law, constitu- tional doctrine, and practices that permit the government to employ these forces.

So imposing an array of coercion in the hands of the government would be a permanent temptation to unscrupulous leaders and a standing danger to all opposition. Although it is conceivable that a popular govern- ment might coerce a large fraction of the population on infrequent occa- sions and survive, the more frequently it did so, the more reduced the chances of its survival would be. For example, when extensive coercion over blacks was reestablished in the American South in the last quarter of the nineteenth century, in effect the South developed a dual political system in which whites operated a quasipolyarchy and black southerners lived under a repressive hegemony.

Reciprocal vs. Unilateral Control.   Because effective rights to opposi- tion and participation are diffused more widely in polyarchies than in non- polyarchies, individuals and groups enjoy more autonomy vis-à-vis the gov- ernment, the opportunities for political leaders to employ coercion against their critics and opponents are more limited, persuasion is more readily available than coercion as a means of influence, and political leaders are more likely to be involved in networks of reciprocal influence. In polyarchies, government policies are likely to be settled by negotiation and bargaining. In authoritarian regimes, by contrast, the influence of leaders is more unilateral, and policies are more likely to be attained by hierarchy and command.

Paths to the Present.   Because the path that each country has taken to the present is unique, every country has a different legacy of conditions bearing on the chances for polyarchy and peaceful adjustment.

In some countries, violent revolutions (particularly revolutionary wars for national independence) have helped to unite a people, while in other countries revolutions have left enduring cleavages. Compare the results of the American Revolution and the creation of the Irish Free State, later the Republic of Ireland. In each case a violent struggle against Britain led to independence. In America, however, the Revolution, the armed struggle against the British, the mass exodus of British colonials, and the development of a widely shared republican ideology helped to foster unifying myths and left few divisive scars among the American people. But in Ireland the peace treaty in 1921 that preserved Protestant North Ireland as an integral part of the United Kingdom led immediately to fierce conflicts between the government of the new Irish Free State and the Irish Republican Army (I.R.A.) and then to persistent and bloody conflict in North Ireland between Protestant Irish and Catholic Irish, with the I.R.A. acting in violent support of the Catholic minority.

In a different perspective, some countries have enjoyed centuries of national independence in the course of which they have been able to accumulate political experience, develop their institutions, generate loyalties, break down cultural cleavages, establish a sense of nationhood, and work out ways of accommodation in their conflicts. Other countries have only recently become independent after decades or centuries of foreign rule and colonialism. These countries are new, still struggling to achieve a national identity, and still passing through the Time of Troubles. Racked by open or potential conflict, still unable, so their elites believe, to afford the luxury of polyarchy, leaders rely heavily on coercion to keep the nation and its institutions intact.

A further question now arises: What factors help to bring about polyarchy—or prevent it? The answer is of more than abstract interest because the differences between polyarchies and nonpolyarchies described in this chapter are important to us. In the next chapter, therefore, we shall attempt to explain why polyarchy has come about in some countries but not in others.

EIGHT

POLYARCHIES
AND NONPOLYARCHIES:
EXPLANATION

As we saw in Figure 7–2, around 30 percent of all the countries in the present world are governed by polyarchal systems. In the 1980s, these countries—democratic countries—numbered about 51 of approximately 170 nominally independent countries in the world. How can we account for the fact that some countries have developed and sustained the institutions of polyarchy while others have not?

HOW VIOLENT COERCION IS EMPLOYED BY RULERS[1]

In Chapter 1 the government of the state was distinguished from other governments by virtue of its success in upholding its claim to the exclusive regulation of the legitimate use of physical force in enforcing its rules within a given territorial area. All states employ coercion or the threat of coercion, internally to enforce laws and policies and often externally in their relations with other states. The typical and distinctive capacities of a

---

[1]For a more extended treatment of the matters discussed in this section and the next, see my *Democracy and Its Critics* (New Haven: Yale University Press, 1989), pp. 244–56.

state are its instruments for violent physical coercion—specifically military and police organizations, including secret police.

What is to prevent leaders from employing coercive violence to intervene in political life, impede or overthrow the institutions of polyarchy, or establish and maintain an authoritarian regime? Throughout history they have done so. They do so today in many countries.[2]

For a country to be governed by a polyarchy, then, two conditions are required: (1) Military and police organizations must be subject to civilian control, and (2) the civilians who control the military and police must themselves be subject to control by means of the institutions of polyarchy.

The first requirement is greatly eased if the military establishment is feeble or nonexistent, as it was in many countries during the emergence of polyarchy in the nineteenth century. For the first century and a half of its national existence, for example, the United States maintained only a tiny military establishment during peacetime. In rare cases, a military establishment may not even exist. Thus after a brief period when a government took office with the aid of military forces, in Costa Rica the armed forces were literally abolished in 1948–49. Japan, where the military had become a powerful political actor in the 1930s, declared in its 1947 constitution that it would never maintain land, sea, and air forces. Although the provision was weakened by the subsequent development of a national "police reserve" and then a "national defense force," its effect was to prevent the reemergence of the military as a significant political actor in the new polyarchy.

Most countries, however, do have a military establishment of some importance. In 1983 the world average for military expenditures was 5.6 percent of a country's gross national product.[3] Most countries possess military forces powerful enough to prevail over civilians in a straight-out violent confrontation. And as Figure 8–1 shows, in many countries the military has in fact successfully intervened in politics to establish a government more acceptable to military leaders. In the fifteen-year period from 1958 to 1973, governments were affected by military intervention in more than one out of every three countries.

What restrains the military forces in some countries from taking control of their governments away from civilian leaders? Military professionalism sometimes helps by creating and sustaining beliefs about the regime to which the military owes loyalty and obedience and to which it is obligated. Yet professionalism does not ensure civilian control, much less democratic

[2]For the role of the military in politics today, see S. E. Finer, *The Man on Horseback: The Role of the Military in Politics,* 2nd ed. (Boulder, Colo.: Westview Press and London: Pinter Publishers, 1988); Eric A. Nordlinger, *Soldiers in Politics: Military Coups and Governments* (Englewood Cliffs, N.J.: Prentice-Hall, 1977); Amos Perlmutter, *The Military and Politics in Modern Times* (New Haven, Conn.: Yale University Press, 1977); Samuel P. Huntington, *The Soldier and the State* (Cambridge, Mass.: Harvard University Press, 1957).

[3]Ruth Leger Sivard, *World Military and Social Expenditures,* 11th ed. (Washington D.C.: World Priorities, 1986), Table 2, pp. 33 ff.

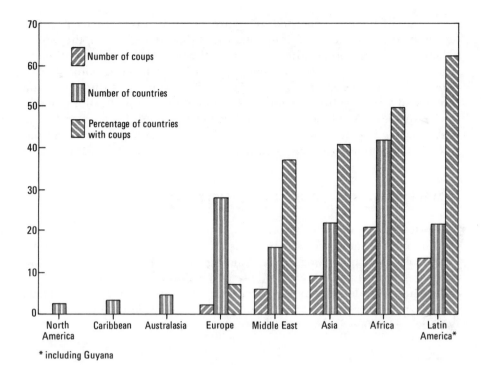

* including Guyana

FIGURE 8-1. Successful military coups by world regions, 1958–1973. Source: S. E. Finer, *The Man on Horseback: The Role of the Military in Politics,* 2nd ed. (Boulder, Colo.: Westview Press, 1988), p. 312.

control. For professionalism may also create a deep social and psychological gulf between military professionals and civilians, so that the military becomes a distinctly separate caste cut off from civilian society. Moreover, military professionals may resist civilian control or cast it off entirely if they believe that civilian leaders endanger the military establishment. And they may also reject civilian control if they believe that the stability, health, or existence of the system or the values they are obligated to preserve—the social order, the economic system, religion, national independence, for example—is endangered by the civilian leaders.[4]

What is more, while civilian control is a necessary condition for polyarchy, as the second requirement mentioned earlier indicates, civilian control is clearly not sufficient. After all, many authoritarian regimes are ruled by civilian leaders who employ the military or the police or both to stamp out resistance to their rule. Obviously, then, polyarchy requires other conditions as well.

[4]For instances of each, see Alfred Stepan, *The Military in Politics: Changing Patterns in Brazil* (Princeton, N.J.: Princeton University Press, 1971) and "The New Professionalism of Internal Warfare and Military Role Expansion," in Alfred Stepan, ed., *Authoritarian Brazil* (New Haven, Conn.: Yale University Press, 1973), pp. 47–65. Eric Nordlinger, *Soldiers in Politics: Military Coups and Governments* (Englewood Cliffs, N.J.: Prentice-Hall, 1977).

One of these is suggested by Figure 8-1, which reveals sharp differences in the likelihood of coups among different regions of the world. These regional differences in turn point to the possible importance of political cultures, ideas, beliefs, attitudes. We shall return to this point shortly. Another difference is indicated in Figure 8-2. The lower the per capita income of a country, the greater the likelihood of a coup. It is not immediately obvious why this should be so. But the relationship shown in Figure 8-2 is a part of a much more pervasive relationship between polyarchy and the socioeconomic order of a country.

A MODERN, DYNAMIC, PLURALIST SOCIETY

Historically, polyarchy has been strongly associated with a society marked by a number of interrelated characteristics: a relatively high level of income and wealth per capita, long-run economic growth, urbanization, a small and declining agricultural population, literacy, widespread education, a variety of relatively independent organizations such as business firms, trade unions, churches, and so on, and high levels of conventional indicators of well-being, such as infant mortality and life expectancy.

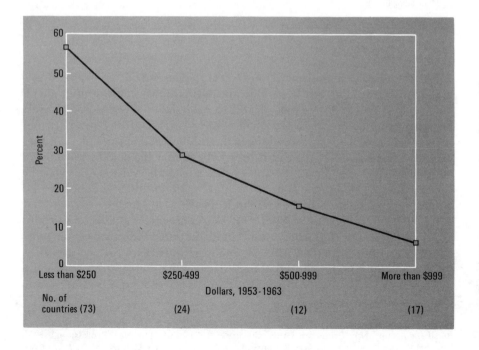

FIGURE 8-2. Per capita income and percentage of coups, 1958–1973. Source: Finer, p. 313.

Societies like these have been called liberal, capitalist, bourgeois, middle-class, business, industrial, advanced industrial (and post industrial), modern (and postmodern), competitive, market-oriented, open, and so on. They are *modern* in the sense of historically high levels of wealth and income, consumption, education, urbanization, and other features: *dynamic* by virtue of their rates of economic growth and increasing standards of living; and *pluralist* because of the existence of many relatively independent groups, associations, organizations, and other units. They might then be called *modern dynamic pluralist societies* (or for short, MDP societies).

To see how an MDP society strongly favors polyarchy, it is helpful to arrange the countries of the world according to how fully they possess the institutions of polyarchy. In Figure 8–3 163 countries are classified into 13 categories. The first category consists of countries where all the institutions of polyarchy existed in the mid-1980s. These countries are, however, divided into two groups: (I.A) countries in which the institutions had existed steadily since at least 1950 (old or stable polyarchies) and (I.B) countries in which they had not (new polyarchies).[5] In the other categories, with one important exception the countries are ranked by the extent to which four of the major institutions of polyarchy were present: access to alternative sources of information, freedom of expression, freedom of organization, and free and fair elections. For example, in countries of category II one of these institutions was below the threshold of the polyarchies; at the other extreme in countries classified in category X, all the institutions of polyarchy were virtually nonexistent. One important group of countries, consisting of the Soviet Union and the countries of eastern Europe, comprise a special category. Although in the mid-1980s, most were in the last category (X) and a few (Poland, Hungary) in a somewhat higher one, because of the rapid and dramatic changes taking place in these countries during the last half of that decade, they occupy a special place. I shall say more about them in a moment.

As we saw in the last chapter, GNP per capita is a rough and ready indicator of an MDP society because it is associated with so many of its features. Figure 8–4 shows that almost all the older polyarchal democracies are among the top fifth of the countries in GNP per capita. Three out of the four wealthiest countries are either old or new polyarchies. Conversely, none of the poorest countries—the bottom fifth in Figure 8–4—is a polyarchy.

If we ignore the Soviet Union and Eastern Europe, the stronger the indicators of an MDP society, the greater the likelihood that a country will possess the institutions of polyarchy. Conversely, of course, the weaker the

[5]Thus some are new countries, some are newly democratized, and in some polyarchy was reestablished after a period of authoritarian rule.

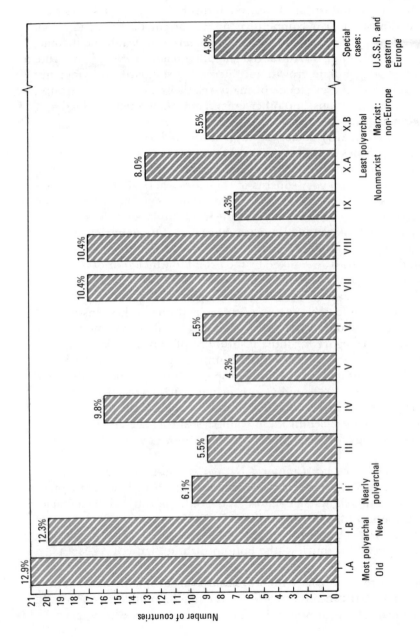

FIGURE 8–3. 163 countries classified by extent to which four institutions of polyarchy existed, mid-1980s. Percentages are percent of total countries. Sources: Michael Coppedge and Wolfgang Reinicke, "A Measure of Polyarchy," paper prepared for the Conference on Measuring Democracy, Hoover Institution, Stanford University, May 27–28, 1988. I have removed the U.S.S.R. and eastern European countries from their classification and treated them as special cases.

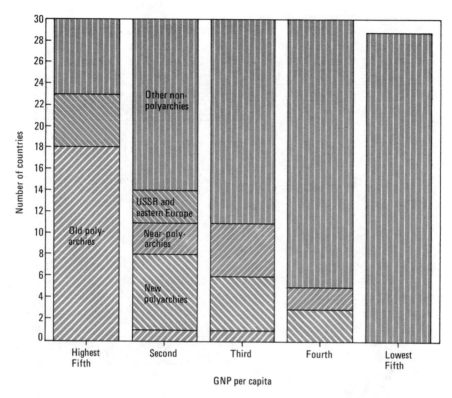

FIGURE 8-4. GNP per capita and the frequency of polyarchy (149 countries). Sources: For GNP, see sources cited in Table 6.2. For political classification, see Figure 8-3.

indicators are, the weaker the institutions of polyarchy are also likely to be. As Figure 8–5 reveals, however, high per capita income does not automatically generate polyarchy, and relatively low income per capita does not necessarily prevent it. Aside from eastern Europe, the exceptional countries in Figure 8–5 are the suddenly rich oil states of the Middle East, which have largely retained their traditional forms of rule. Other indicators of an MDP society show an even more consistent relationship (Figures 8-6–8-7).

What explains this relationship? So many characteristics of an MDP society are favorable to polyarchy that it is a mistake to focus on one, like GNP, as primary or causal. The multiplicity of favorable aspects may be reduced to two general features: (1) An MDP society disperses power, influence, authority, and control away from any single center toward a variety of individuals, groups, associations, and organizations, and (2) it fosters attitudes and beliefs favorable to democratic ideas.[6]

[6]See Ronald Inglehart, *Culture Shift in Advanced Industrial Society* (Princeton, N.J.: Princeton University Press, 1989), Chap. 1.

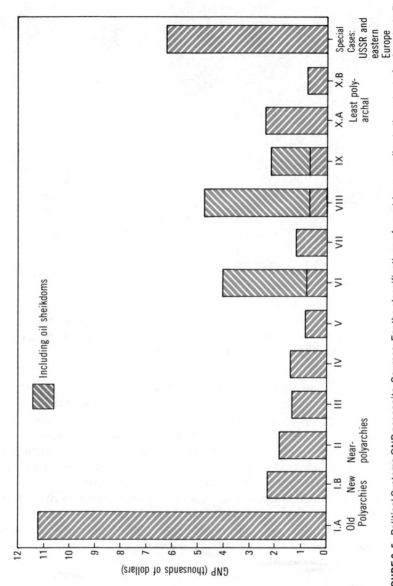

FIGURE 8–5. Political Systems-GNP per capita. Sources: For the classifications of countries according to the extent of polyarchy in Figures 8–5 to 8–8, see Figure 8–3. For GNP per capita, education, literacy, number of persons per physician, and infant mortality in these figures, see the sources for Table 6–2.

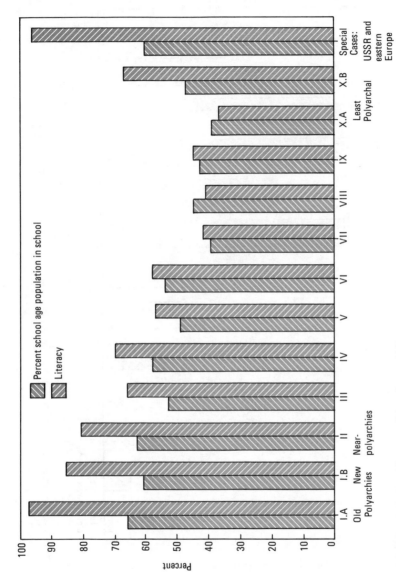

FIGURE 8-6. Political Systems: Education and Literacy

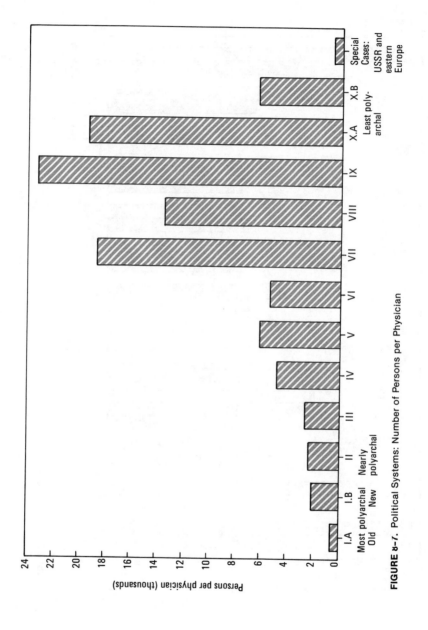

FIGURE 8-7. Political Systems: Number of Persons per Physician

Thus as an authoritarian country acquires the characteristics of an MDP society, it also generates internal pressure—social, economic, cultural, psychological, political—for the introduction and strengthening of rights, liberties, and opportunities: to seek information from nongovernmental sources, to express one's beliefs, to organize independent political, cultural, social, and economic movements, and to participate in free and fair elections of the top officials of government. To repress the movement toward change becomes more difficult and costly for the leadership. A discrepancy exists between the authoritarian political system and the emerging character of the society.

By the 1980s, the Soviet Union and eastern European countries were taking on many of the characteristics of MDP societies, as can be seen from Figures 8–3 through 8–8. A profound discrepancy existed between their highly authoritarian regimes and the pressures generated by their nascent MDP societies. In Poland and Hungary restrictions on information, expression, and organization were already fewer than in the Soviet Union. When Gorbachev assumed leadership of the Soviet Union in 1985 and advanced a program calling for greater openness and more democratic practices in government, the underlying and hitherto largely repressed forces burst into public view, and the political system of the Soviet Union began to move closer to polyarchy.

That a strong association exists between full polyarchy and a highly developed MDP society is hardly open to doubt. But if the explanation is to be found in the two features mentioned earlier, then it follows that if those two features were produced by a different society, then that society would also be favorable to polyarchy. The twenty-one countries where the institutions of polyarchy have existed since at least 1950—the older or stable polyarchies in Figure 8–3—did not have MDP societies when these institutions took root and developed. The United States, for example, was overwhelmingly agricultural. If we were to rely on the kinds of indicators shown in the figures we might conclude that polyarchy was most unlikely in the United States. Yet its agrarian society did possess the two crucial features, at least among white males: It dispersed power and influence very broadly among white males, and it fostered among them beliefs favorable to democracy. Although agrarian societies like those of nineteenth-century America, Canada, Australia, New Zealand, Norway, Sweden, and Switzerland are unlikely to reappear, they serve to remind us that an MDP society is not strictly necessary for polyarchy.

Strong as the association appears to be, then, the deviations in both directions tell us that other factors must be at work. Earlier we examined one of these—the control of the military and police. Another that needs to be taken into account is the way that subcultures may affect political life.

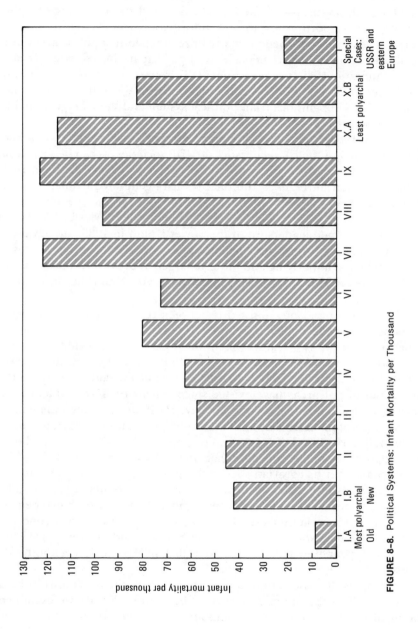

FIGURE 8-8. Political Systems: Infant Mortality per Thousand

SUBCULTURES[7]

As we have seen, countries differ in the extent to which the past has left a legacy of subcultural differences in religion, ethnic groupings, race, and language, and of memories of past treatment of these differences. Both aspects are important. The level of consensus in a country, and hence the chances of peaceful adjustment and polyarchy, are influenced both by the degree of subcultural diversity and by the way that differences in subcultures are dealt with. A legacy of subcultural differences increases the area of potential conflict. The fact that New Zealand, Sweden, Norway, and Iceland are culturally quite homogeneous helps to account for their relatively low levels of conflict. Conversely, India's innumerable subcultures contribute heavily to its high level of conflict. It is not surprising, then, that polyarchies are much more common in homogeneous countries than in countries with numerous subculture cleavages.

But the ways in which countries deal with their subcultural differences also help to explain levels of agreement and conflict. If the level of conflicts is higher in Belgium than in Switzerland, for example, much of the explanation can be found in the fact that Switzerland, with four language groups, two religions, and strong cantonal loyalties, has managed to avoid serious discrimination among its subcultures. By contrast, Belgium still suffers from several centuries of discrimination of Walloons against Flemings. The United States, while relatively successful in avoiding conflicts among a people marked by religious and ethnic diversity, has a record unequaled in any other polyarchy of discriminating against inhabitants of African origin, both as slaves and citizens. This legacy of discrimination was a direct cause of the civil strife over the rights and opportunities of African Americans that swept the United States in the 1960s.

The factors discussed in this chapter are by no means the only ones that would be required for a full explanation for polyarchy or its absence. There has been no mention of beliefs, attitudes, ideas, orientations, or political culture, for example. Yet each of these plays a major and independent role. Some aspects of these will be taken up in the next chapter.

Many countries in the world, it is clear, now possess many or all of the conditions necessary for polyarchal democracy to exist. If and as more countries develop these conditions, the likelihood that they will also develop the institutions of polyarchy will increase. Yet in many countries the conditions that favor polyarchy are not likely to come about in the foresee-

---

[7]Some countries have successfully dealt with subcultural cleavages by creating systems of "consociational democracy," in which the political leaders of all significant subcultures participate in a grand coalition in which no decisions affecting the vital interests of any of the subcultures will be taken without the agreement of its leaders. Successful cases include Switzerland, Holland, Belgium, and Austria. For a description and analysis of consociational democracy, see Arend Lijphart, *Democracy in Plural Societies* (New Haven, Conn.: Yale University Press, 1977).

able future, and in these countries political systems other than polyarchy will exist.

There can be no guarantee, certainly, that political conflicts will be settled peacefully, that democratic ideals will be realized more fully, that many new polyarchies will emerge, or even that all existing polyarchies will endure. Yet it is reasonable to hope that as our knowledge about the central questions of this chapter increases, people will be able to act more wisely to reduce coercion, adjust their conflicts peacefully, and improve the performance of governments, as measured against the exacting and unachieved standards of democracy.

NINE
POLITICAL MEN AND WOMEN

A starting point for all political theory is the fact that members of the human species live together. With few exceptions, human beings do not live in complete isolation. Whatever may be the elements of instinct, habit, necessity, or choice that induce people to form societies, they have demonstrated amply for thousands of years that the human being is a social animal. Yet, although they are social animals, neither by instinct nor by learning are they necessarily political animals—at least not in quite the same sense. Even though they live in a society, they need not concern themselves with the politics of that society, nor participate actively in political life, nor cherish the political institutions and values of the society. Some people do but many do not.

Nonetheless, because human beings are social, they develop political systems. Evidently they cannot dwell together without entering into relationships of influence. Whenever these relationships become stable and repetitive, political systems exist.

In this looser sense, then, one might say (with Aristotle) that man *is* a political animal. Whatever their values and concerns, people are inevitably enmeshed in political systems—whether or not they like or even notice the fact.

However, persons who find themselves within the boundaries of a political system are by no means equally concerned with political life. Moreover, a person may be deeply involved in the political life of one system—family, say, or club, workplace, business firm, union, church, school, and so on— and not in the political life that revolves around the government of the state, or what in Chapter 1 was referred to as the Government. Because of the importance of the Government, this chapter mainly focuses on activity involving this particular government. It is to activity surrounding the Government of the State, then, that terms like politics, political life, political attitudes, and so on will refer. You should keep in mind, therefore, that the description and explanation in this chapter do not necessarily apply to activities in spheres other than the Government of the State.

I said a moment ago that people are not equally concerned with political life. This is clearly so in the Government of the State. Some people are indifferent to politics in that sphere; others are deeply involved. Even among those who are heavily involved in politics, only some actively seek power. And among the power seekers, some gain more power than others. These four groups—the apolitical stratum, the political stratum, the power seekers, and the powerful—are shown in Figure 9–1.

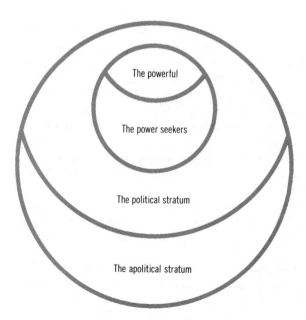

FIGURE 9-1 Political Strata

THE APOLITICAL STRATUM

Since the apolitical stratum shades off imperceptibly into the political stratum, an exact boundary between the two must be arbitrary. Nonetheless, they are, as we shall see, distinguishable.

Because many of us take it for granted that people are naturally political animals, the existence of active and involved citizens, who make up the political stratum, hardly seems to need an explanation. What is more puzzling is the presence of an apolitical stratum.

It appears to be true, nonetheless, that in most countries, those who show great interest in political matters, are concerned and informed about politics, and are active in public affairs do not make up a large proportion of adults; usually, it appears, they are a minority. Even in countries with popular governments where opportunities for political involvement are extensive, the political stratum by no means includes all the citizens. On the contrary, in all polyarchies, it seems, a sizable number of citizens are apathetic about politics and relatively inactive. In short, they are apolitical.

To be sure, there are significant variations from one system to another and from time to time. Yet the failure of a considerable body of citizens to take advantage of opportunities to participate in political life seems to be a nearly universal phenomenon. Even the Greek city-states, which are sometimes held up as models of democratic participation, were not immune.[1]

Sometimes New England town meetings are regarded as models of democratic participation. But just as in Athens, in New England towns many citizens were unconcerned about exercising their rights or fulfilling their political obligations.[2] Even today the problem is acute. In most polyarchies, between a fifth and a third of the eligible voters usually do not vote in

---

[1] The surviving evidence is far too fragmentary to permit firm conclusions and classical scholars differ in their interpretations. From the estimated size of the Athenian citizen body (thirty to forty thousand), the size of a quorum required for some purposes (six thousand), and the estimate of eighteen thousand seats on the Pnyx, where the citizen assembly met, it is reasonable to infer that a substantial percentage of Athenian citizens did not attend the assembly meetings. The figures are from C. M. Bowra, *Classical Greece* (New York: Time Inc., 1965), p. 108, and H. D. F. Kitto, *The Greeks* (Baltimore, Md.: Penguin Books, 1951, 1957), p. 131. For a view that political life in Athens was highly participatory and democratic, see Josiah Ober, *Mass and Elite in Democratic Athens* (Princeton, N.J.: Princeton University Press, 1989).

[2] In New Haven, for example, the problem seems to have been persistent. In 1642 the General Court of the Colony "voted that any freeman who after due warning, should fail to appear in the General Courts before the Secretary finished the roll-call, should be fined 1s, 6d; and that any of the rest of the planters who should be absent after their names were read, should be fined one shilling. The novelty of the first few years had worn away, and attendance at General Courts seemed, to many, burdensome." A century later the problem was still unsolved. Charles H. Levermore, *The Republic of New Haven* (Baltimore, Md.: Johns Hopkins University Press, 1886), pp. 44, 231.

national elections, and much larger fractions abstain from other kinds of political activity.[3]

Why is it that even in modern societies with widespread education, universal suffrage, and democratic political systems the apolitical stratum is so large? To answer this question would require much more space than can be given here, but a short if somewhat formal answer can be given. There seem to be several fundamental reasons why people do not become involved in politics.

(1)*You are less likely to get involved in politics if you place a low value on the rewards expected from political involvement relative to the rewards you expect from other kinds of activity.* The rewards a person may gain (or expect) from political activity can be conveniently divided into two kinds: *direct gratifications* received from the activity itself and *instrumental benefits* brought about as a consequence of the activity.

Direct gratifications from involvement in the Government include the sense of fulfilling one's obligations as a citizen, the pleasures of social interaction with friends and acquaintances, heightened self-esteem from contact with important persons or access to inside information, the excitement of politics as a game or contest in which one's side may win or lose, and so on. For many people, however, political activity is a good deal less gratifying than other outlets—for example, family, recreation, friendships formed at work or in one's neighborhood. For many, involvement in the political life of the State yields far less affection, income, security, respect, excitement, and other values than working at one's job, watching television, reading, fishing, playing with the children, attending a football game, or assembling a new hi-fi set. The explanation, no doubt, lies in the fact that people are not by instinct reasonable, reasoning, civic-minded beings. Many of our most imperious desires and the source of many of our most powerful gratifications can be traced to ancient and persistent biological and physiological drives, needs, and wants. Organized political life arrived late in human evolution; today people learn how to behave as political participants with the aid, and often with the hindrance, of instinctive equipment that is the product of a long development. To avoid pain, discomfort, and hunger, to satisfy drives for sexual gratification, love, security, and respect are insistent and primordial needs. The means of satisfying them quickly and concretely generally lie outside political life.[4]

---

[3]Rates for various forms of participation in a number of countries can be found in Ronald Inglehart, *Culture Shift in Advanced Industrial Society* (Princeton,N.J.: Princeton University Press, 1989), Chap. 10. C. Bingham Powell, Jr., "American Voter Turnout in Comparative Perspective", *American Political Science Review* 80, no. 1 (March 1986), pp. 18–43. Sidney Verba, Norman H. Nie, and Jae-on Kim, *Participation and Political Equality: A Sseven-Nation Comparison* (Cambridge, Mass.: Cambridge University Press, 1978). Gabriel A. Almond and Sidney Verba, *The Civic Culture* (Boston: Little, Brown & Company, 1965), Table II.5, p. 56.

[4]Robert E. Lane compares money and power as sources of satisfaction and addiction in

Instrumental benefits expected from political activity may be divided roughly into two kinds. Some are special benefits for a particular person or family—a job from party leaders, pay for being a pollwatcher, graft, and so on. Or the benefits may be favorable government decisions: "the government issues a zoning variance to an individual so that he can enlarge his home, provides a license, grants an exemption from the army because of a family hardship, removes an unsightly telephone pole, offers agricultural assistance or agrees to provide a better water supply to a given home."[5] For some people, special benefits provide a sufficient incentive for political participation. The old-fashioned American political machine built the loyalty of its followers and party workers essentially on special benefits.

But particularized benefits rarely are extended widely enough to involve the whole citizen body. All that most citizens hope to gain from government are collective benefits (costs)—consequences of decisions that affect a large category of persons such as taxpayers, social security beneficiaries, automobile drivers, and so on. In decisions about war and peace, foreign affairs, military policy, and a number of other matters, the collectivity may include virtually the whole citizen body. However, some people do not believe that they stand to benefit from these governmental activities. In a survey of political attitudes and activities of citizens in four polyarchies and one regime dominated by a single party (Mexico), about three-quarters of the people in the United States and Britain thought the activities of the national government tended to improve conditions in the area, about half thought the same in Germany and Italy, and a sixth in Mexico. The rest were in varying degrees hostile, doubtful, uncertain, or without an opinion.[6] For some persons, then, the rewards of political involvement are distant and vague, whereas the rewards of other activities are more immediate and concrete.

In short, for many people the opportunity costs of political involvement are simply too high to make it worthwhile. These people are unwilling to forego immediate, certain, and concrete benefits or gratifications derived from nonpolitical activities to obtain the more remote, uncertain, and abstract benefits that might ensue from political participation.

(2) *You are less likely to get involved in politics if you think that there is no significant difference in the alternatives before you and, consequently, that what you do won't matter.* Thus people who say they don't care "which party wins the presidential election this fall" are much less likely to vote in American presi-

"Experiencing Money and Experiencing Power," in Ian Shapiro and Grant Reeher, *Power, Inequality , and Democratic Politics* (Boulder, Colo.: Westview Press, 1988), pp. 80–105.

[5]Sidney Verba and Norman H. Nie, *Participation in America* (New York: Harper and Row, 1972), p. 49. The distinction between the two forms of participation described in this and the following paragraph is taken from Verba's and Nie's discussion.

[6]Gabriel A. Almond and Sidney Verba, *The Civic Culture* (Boston: Little, Brown & Company, 1965), Table II.3, p. 48

dential elections than those who say they care a good deal.[7] Some people fail to vote or otherwise participate in politics because they believe the candidates or parties do not offer them a real choice.

(3) *You are less likely to become involved in politics if you think that what you do won't matter because you can't significantly change the outcome anyway.* A great many surveys have demonstrated a strong relationship between the confidence that what one does really matters and the extent of one's political involvement. The weaker one's "sense of political efficacy," the less likely one is to become involved.[8]

The confidence one has in one's capacity to be effective in political life depends on many factors. Confidence may, of course, reflect a realistic appraisal of a situation. It is hardly surprising that people who see an upcoming election as a completely one-sided affair are less likely to vote than those who believe that it is going to be close. Even people who care a great deal about the outcome of an election may decide not to vote if they believe that the election is too one-sided for their vote to make any difference.[9] Nor should it be too surprising that in a number of countries people are likely to have more confidence in their capacity to be effective in changing the conduct of government at the local level than at the national level.[10]

Whether the judgment is realistic or not, many citizens are weighed

---

[7]The relationship between voting and concern was first reported for American voters in the classical study by Angus Campbell, Philip E. Converse, Warren E. Miller, and Donald Stokes, *The American Voter* (New York: John Wiley & Sons, Inc., 1960), p. 104. Since their work, some scholars have argued that a decline in concern among American voters as to which party wins has contributed substantially to a decline in voter turnout in presidential elections. Other scholars argue, however, that because the relationship between concern and turnout is moderate, and the decline in concern is also moderate, more important factors must be involved. Cf. Paul R. Abramson and John H. Aldrich, "The Decline of Electoral Participation in America," *American Political Science Review* 76, no. 3 (September 1982), p. 519; and Carol A. Cassel and Robert C. Luskin, "Simple Explanations of Turnout Decline," *American Political Science Review* 82, no. 4 (December 1988), p. 1325.

[8]For the effects of political efficacy on voter turnout in nine countries, see Powell, "American Voter Turnout," Table 4, p. 30.

[9]The hypothesis that elections in which contests are one-sided reduce voters' incentive to vote, while close races increase their incentive, has a long history and is a matter of continuing scholarly controversy and discussion. In 1930, Harold F. Gosnell found that British elections confirmed the hypothesis–*Why Europe Votes* (Chicago: University of Chicago Press, 1930), p. 14. In their seminal study, Campbell et al. found it also held true in American presidential elections. (*The American Voter pp. 516–19*). Later studies have shown, however, that in the United States campaign spending also increases in electoral districts where contests are close. Presumably greater expenditures cause greater turnout. Nonetheless, closeness of elections does appear to have some effect on voters' incentive to turn out in the United States. See, for example, Samuel C. Patterson and Gregory A. Caldeira, "Getting Out the Vote: Participation in Gubernatorial Elections," *American Political Science Review* 77, no. 3 (September 1983), pp. 675–89; Gary W. Cox and Michael C. Munger, "Closeness, Expenditures, and Turnout in the 1982 U.S. House Elections," *American Political Science Review* 83, no. 1 (March 1989), pp. 217–31. The extent to which the relation exists in other countries is, however, unclear. See Powell "American Voter Turnout," and Robert W. Jackman, "Political Institutions and Voter Turnout in the Industrial Democracies," *American Political Science Review* 81, no. 2 (June 1987), pp. 405–24.

[10]Robert A. Dahl and Edward R. Tufte, *Size and Democracy* (Stanford, Calif.: Stanford University Press, 1973), pp. 53–65.

down by a sense that officials just won't pay attention "to people like me." In the United States, political self-confidence—the sense of political efficacy—tends to increase the higher one's income, social standing, political experience, and, most of all, education.

Probably one's "personality" has some bearing on one's sense of efficacy. Optimism or pessimism about one's chances of influencing policy probably is related to deeper personality factors, such as an underlying sense of confidence that pervades a person's entire outlook.[11] One's political confidence, or lack of it, may feed on itself. A person lacking in confidence may avoid politics, thus decreasing one's chances of being effective and further diminishing one's confidence. Conversely, a confident person may, as a result of political involvement, grow even more confident.

(4) *You are less likely to become involved in politics if you believe that the outcome will be relatively satisfactory to you without your involvement.* A citizen who believes a particular political decision is important, nevertheless might not become involved in it if he or she feels quite confident that the decision will turn out well anyway. Just as low confidence in one's political efficacy discourages participation, so too, high confidence in the all-round justice legitimacy, stability, and fairness of decisions in one's political system may make one's participation seem unnecessary.

(5) *You are less likely to get involved in politics if you feel that your knowledge is too limited for you to be effective.* In every country, it seems, large numbers of people feel they do not understand politics very well.[12] It is not surprising that some of them turn away from politics entirely.

(6) *Finally, the greater the obstacles placed in your way, the less likely you are to become involved in politics.* When people expect high rewards from an activity, they are willing to overcome great obstacles and incur high "costs" to gain them. But when they believe the rewards are going to be low or non-existent, even modest obstacles and costs are enough to discourage them. Why bother to climb over a fence if the grass is not greener on the other side?

Thus there is good reason for thinking that the markedly low turnout in national elections in the United States, as compared with almost all other countries, is caused partly by an additional barrier to voting—registration requirements. In other countries citizens do not have to "register" or may do so in a simple, convenient, almost automatic way. In the United States, differences in registration procedures and requirements tend to effect the percentage of the population of voting age that registers.[13]

---

[11]Campbell et al., *The American Voter,* pp. 516–19.

[12]Dahl and Tufte, *Size and Democracy* Table 4.8, p. 54.

[13]Steven J. Rosenstone and Raymond E. Wolfinger, *Who Votes?* (New Haven, Conn.: Yale University Press, 1981). From his comparative study of nine countries, Powell concludes that "if the United States adopted automatic registration, or something similar, turnout might be increased by 14%." ("American Voter Turnout," p. 35.)

The costs of politcal involvement also may vary with different activities. As Verba and Nie have emphasized, some activities, such as campaigning, involve conflict with other participants; people who dislike conflict, then, are more likely to stay away from these forms of participation. In addition, they point out, some activities—getting in touch with an official, for example—require much more initiative than does voting.[14] It is hardly surprising that voting is far more common than citizen-initiated contacts with officials.

THE POLITICAL STRATUM

All the forces we have just examined also can work in reverse. It seems obvious that you are *more* likely to become involved in politics if you:

1. value the rewards to be gained
2. think the alternatives are important
3. are confident that you can help to change the outcome
4. believe the outcome will be unsatisfactory if you don't act
5. have knowledge or skill that bears on the question at hand
6. must overcome fewer obstacles to act.

Because of these and other factors, some people *are* interested in politics, *are* concerned and informed about politics, and *do* participate in political life. These people constitute the political stratum.

Yet the same forces seem to operate within the political stratum: Some people are much more interested, concerned, informed, and active than others. In countries with popular governments in which citizens are legally free to participate in a wide variety of political acts, the more demanding, the more time-consuming, costly, or difficult the activities are, the smaller are the numbers who engage in them. Citizens are much more likely to vote, for example, than to attend a political meeting, more likely to attend a meeting than to work actively for a candidate or party. Few citizens try to influence an act of the national legislature or, for that matter, the more accessible officials of the local government (see Table 9–1). In the most complete study of political participation among Americans (see Table 9–2), Verba and Nie have shown that "voting in Presidential elections is the only participatory act out of our rather extensive list of activities that is performed by a majority of those interviewed."[15]

In addition, however, Verba and Nie discovered a phenomenon that had been largely overlooked in previous studies of participation: There is a significant degree of specialization within the political stratum. They

[14]Verba and Nie, *Participation in America*, pp. 50–51.
[15]Verba and Nie, *Participation in America*, p. 31.

TABLE 9-1   Percentage Who Say They Have Attempted to Influence the Government (by Country)

COUNTRY	LOCAL GOVERNMENT[a]	NATIONAL LEGISLATURE[b]	N
U.S.	28%	16%	970
U.K.	15	6	963
Germany	14	3	955
Italy	8	2	995
Mexico	6	3	1295

[a]"Have you ever done anything to try to influence a local decision?"
[b]"Have you ever done anything to try to influence an act of the [national legislature]?"
Source: Almond and Verba survey, unpublished data.

TABLE 9-2   Percentage of Americans Engaging in Twelve Different Acts of Political Participation

TYPE OF POLITICAL PARTICIPATION	PERCENTAGE
1. Report regularly voting in Presidential elections	72
2. Report always voting in local elections	47
3. Active in at least one organization involved in community problems	32
4. Have worked with others in trying to solve some community problems	30
5. Have attempted to persuade others to vote as they were	28
6. Have ever actively worked for a party or candidates during an election	26
7. Have ever contacted a local government official about some issue or problem	20
8. Have attended at least one political meeting or rally in last three years	19
9. Have ever contacted a state or national government official about some issue or problem	18
10. Have ever formed a group or organization to attempt to solve some local community problem	14
11. Have ever given money to a party or candidate during an election campaign	13
12. Presently a member of a political club or organization	8

Source: Sidney Verba and Norman H. Nie, *Participation in America: Political Democracy and Social Equality,* Table 2-1, p. 31. Copyright © 1972 by Sidney Verba and Norman H. Nie. Reprinted by permission of Harper & Row, Publishers, Inc.

found that Americans could be divided into six types, ranging from the inactives (22 percent) who take "almost no part in political life" (equivalent to our apolitical stratum) to the complete activists (11 percent) who "engage in all types of activity with great frequency."[16]

Thus the members of the political stratum are far from a homogeneous lot. They differ enormously not only in the volume but also in the form of their participation in political life. While it is true that the complete activists are a comparatively small minority in every country, the Verba and Nie findings do show that half of all American citizens engage in some kind of political activity in addition to voting. Altogether, the political stratum in the United States appears to consist of about three-quarters of the adult population.

THE INFLUENCE SEEKERS

Within the political stratum some persons seek to influence the government of the state much more vigorously than others. But to seek influence and to gain it are by no means the same thing. Not only are some influence seekers unsuccessful in their efforts, but some people who acquire influence may not actually seek it—they might gain it by inheritance, for example. In short, within the political stratum there is a substratum of influence seekers and a substratum of influential leaders.

You may notice that what we have just said is a restatement of two propositions set forth in Chapter 6 as empirical characteristics of political systems:

1. Some members of the political system seek to gain influence over the policies, rules, and decisions enforced by the government.
2. Political influence is distributed unevenly among the members of a political system.

We have, then, two important questions. Why do some people seek influence and power more actively than others? Why do some gain more influence and power than others?

Social Characteristics

Although no general answer is possible, certain social characteristics tend to be associated with higher levels of political activity in countries governed by democratic polyarchies. Thus the level of political activity tends to be higher among:

---

[16]Verba and Nie, *Participation in America,* pp. 79–80.

more educated persons
men
people of higher socioeconomic status
older persons'
executives, professionals, and other white-collar workers.[17]

Why do people with these social characteristics tend to participate more in political life? Because persons with characteristics like these also tend to possess greater political resources, skills, and incentives than others; participation is easier and less costly; the perceived rewards (though not necessarily the actual or potential rewards) are greater, the penalties fewer. (In a moment we shall consider the impact of just one characteristic: gender.)

Motives

Yet, important as it is, differences in socioeconomic status explain only a small part of the variation in political activity. Among persons of similar socioeconomic status and similar amounts of resources, some engage far more actively than others in the search for influence over the Government of the State.[18] Why?

The answers can be grouped into three categories.

(1) *People seek to gain influence over the Government,* it is sometimes said, *in order to achieve the general good.* They wish to protect the interest of all citizens, achieve justice for all, benefit the state, or provide for life, liberty, and the pursuit of happiness. This is the argument attributed to Socrates in Plato's *Republic:*

> No science of any kind seeks or orders its own advantage, but that of the weaker which is subject to it and governed by it.

[17]For characteristics associated with participation in various countries, see Inglehart, *Culture Shift,* (12 countries) and Powell, "American Voter Turnout, (11 countries). See also Sidney Verba, Norman H. Nie, and Jae-on Kim, *Participation and Political Equality: A Seven Nation Comparison* (Cambridge, England: Cambridge University Press, 1978). Verba and Nie found a higher correlation between socioeconomic status and participation in the United States than in nine other countries (*Participation in America,* Table 20–1, p. 340.) However, socioeconomic status accounted for less than one-fifth the total variation, leaving 80 percent or more unexplained. Moreover, Rosenstone and Wolfinger, in *Who Votes?,* found that in voting, education was far and away the most important component of socioeconomic status. In fact, they found that among voters with about the same level of education, occupation and income mattered very little.

[18]One should keep in mind the admonitions in Chapter 4 about the absence of standard terminology concerning power and influence, and the difficulties and ambiguities in interpreting the meaning of these concepts. While the concern here is about attempts to gain influence over the Government of the State, discussions bearing on this subject, some of which are referred to below, may focus more explicitly on "ruling" or extend much more widely to seeking "power" in any sphere. In the sections below, I follow the usage of the author when this seems appropriate.

[Thrasymachus] tried to fight this conclusion, but he agreed to this too in the end. And after he had, I said: Surely no physician either, in so far as he is a physician, seeks or orders what is advantageous to himself, but to his patient?
. . .
He said yes . . .
Does it not follow that the ship's captain and ruler will not seek and order what is advantageous to himself, but to the sailor, his subject?
He agreed, but barely.
So then, Thrasymachus, I said, no other ruler in any kind of government, in so far as he is a ruler, seeks what is to his own advantage or orders it, but that which is to the advantage of his subject who is the concern of his craft; it is this he keeps in view; all his words and deeds are directed to this end.[19]

The difficulty with this debate between Socrates (or Plato) and Thrasymachus is that the two men are talking right past one another. This often happens in political controversy; each opponent vigorously flails an argument the other did not make, and thereby fails to meet head-on the precise point the other did make. In this case Socrates evidently intends his argument to be primarily *normative,* while Thrasymachus pretty clearly means his observation to be essentially *empirical.* Socrates met Thrasymachus's attempt to describe how rulers generally *do* act by indicating how good rulers *ought* to act.

Socrates and Plato knew perfectly well that rulers of states do not in fact always rule in the interests of their subjects. Indeed, to both Socrates and Plato the very meaning of a bad or perverted state was that the rulers did not seek the good of those over whom they ruled. Later on in the *Republic,* after describing how dictatorship evolves from democracy, Plato undertakes to explain how "the dictatorial man himself" develops:

. . . Some of our unnecessary pleasures and desires seem to me lawless; they are probably present in everyone, but they are held in check by the laws and by the better desires with the help of reason. In a few men they have been eliminated or a small number are left in a weakened state, while in others they are stronger and more numerous.
. . . What we want to establish is this: that there is a dangerous, wild, and lawless kind of desire in everyone, even the few of us who appear moderate. . . .
This, my dear friend, I said, is precisely how a man becomes dictatorial, when his nature or his pursuits or both make him intoxicated, lustful, and mad.[20]

In sum, many political philosophers have argued that leaders *should* seek to rule in order to exercise authority for the good of all. But probably

---

[19]*Plato's Republic,* trans. by G. M. A. Grube (Indianapolis: Hackett Publishing Co., 1974), lines 342d–43.
[20]*Ibid.,* lines 571b, 572b, and 573c.

no student of politics has ever really argued that this is the only reason, or even the principal reason, why people *do* in fact seek to rule.

(2) *People seek to gain influence over the Government,* it has been argued, *in conscious pursuit of their self-interest.* This was the argument of Thrasymachus that Socrates purported to attack. Thrasymachus had said (according to Plato):

> I say that the just is nothing else than the advantage of the stronger.... Do you not know ... that some cities are ruled by a despot, others by the people, and others again by the aristocracy? ... Yes, and each government makes laws to its own advantage: democracy makes democratic laws, a despotism makes despotic laws, and so with the others, and when they have made these laws they declare this to be just to their subjects, that is, their own advantage, and they punish him who transgresses the laws as lawless and unjust. This then, my good man, is what I say justice is, the same in all cities, the advantage of the established government, and correct reasoning will conclude that the just is the same everywhere, the advantage of the stronger.[21]

Thrasymachus may have represented an early Greek attempt to find naturalistic explanations for political behavior. Since nearly all we know of him comes from his enemy Plato, his argument in the *Republic* probably is somewhat distorted. Evidently Thrasymachus was trying to explain how it is that although rulers always proclaim that they are seeking justice, different rulers impose different ideas of justice on their states. To Thrasymachus the obvious explanation of the paradox was that each ruler was simply pursuing his own self-interest: "Justice" as it was actually defined in the laws of each state was a mere ideological rationalization for the self-interest of the rulers. It is quite possible that Thrasymachus used his analysis to uphold traditional Athenian democratic institutions against subversion by supporters of oligarchy who insisted that they and they alone were concerned for the good of the state. Undoubtedly he also employed his analysis to undermine the appeal of Plato's elaborate defense of aristocracy, which Thrasymachus probably believed was no more than a brilliant rationalization for the antidemocratic ambitions of the oligarchical faction in Athens.[22]

Thrasymachus's hypothesis that people deliberately seek to rule for reasons of self-interest has been restated many times. Hobbes, for example, held that people were impelled by their passions and guided by their reason. Passion is the wind that fills the sails, reason the hand on the rudder. A human being, to use another metaphor, is a chariot pulled by the wild horses of passion and steered by reason. Human desires are insatiable, but reason dictates prudence. With the aid of reason, people can discover the

[21]*Ibid.*, lines 338c, d, e.
[22]On this point see Eric A. Havelock, *The Liberal Temper in Greek Politics* (New Haven, Conn.: Yale University Press, 1957), p. 231 and *passim.*

general rules or precepts that will enable them to improve their chances of gaining the ends their passions dictate. All people, then, seek power in order to satisfy their passions. But reasons tells them *how* to seek power to reduce frustration, defeat, and the chances of violent death.

One difficulty with this hypothesis, as Plato rightly saw, is that the notion of "self-interest," which seems transparently obvious, is actually very complex. What one views as one's "self" depends on one's identifications, and evidently these vary a good deal. How one perceives the self is not wholly instinctive, it seems, but also a matter of social learning and personal development.[23] Likewise, what one considers to be in the "interest" of the self is shaped by learning, experience, tradition, and culture. Consequently, to attribute an act to self-interest does not explain very much. As a distinguished modern psychologist has said:

> The self comprises all the precious things and persons who are relevant to an individual's life, so that the term selfish loses its original connotation, and the proposition that man is selfish resolves itself into the circular statement that people are concerned with the things they are concerned with.[24]

Jones's self-interest can mean his pursuit of advantages for himself alone. Or it can mean his attempt to obtain advantages of all kinds for himself and his family. The Jones family now becomes the "self," and its "interests" run from acquisitiveness to zoology. Or Jones's self-interest can mean his attempt to obtain advantages for larger strata with which he identifies—his neighborhood, region, class, religion, ethnic group, race, nation. Thus both the "self" with which Jones identifies and the range of ends he regards as in the "interests" of the self may be extremely narrow or very wide, depending on learning, experience, tradition, and culture. Anthropological studies testify to the fact that notions of self, interest, and self-interest vary widely among human beings.

A second objection to rational self-interest as an explanation is posed by post-Freudian psychology. Thrasymachus, Hobbes, Bentham, and Marx all interpreted the search for power as "rational" and conscious pursuit of self-interest. But Freud showed that the "dangerous, wild, and lawless kind of" desires of which Socrates spoke do more than drive human beings into

---

[23]Psychologists such as Jean Piaget and his followers, who have carefully observed children, have concluded that the child's "ego" develops naturally through certain stages. See Piaget, *The Moral Judgment of the Child* (New York: The Free Press, 1948), and Erik Erikson, *Childhood and Society* (New York: Norton, 1950). The psychologist Lawrence Kohlberg contends further that human beings have a built-in predisposition to develop their moral understanding through certain stages. See his *The Philosophy of Moral Development,* Vol. I (San Francisco: Harper & Row Publishers, Inc., 1981), and below, Chap. 9, fn. 31, p. 136.

[24]Gardner Murphy, "Social Motivation," in *Handbook of Social Psychology,* vol. 2 ed. G. Lindzey (Reading, Mass.: Addison-Wesley Publishing Co., Inc., 1954), p. 625.

conflict with one another (as Hobbes argued); they also drive human beings into conflict with themselves. These inner conflicts, according to Freud, are fierce gales that often blow out the flickering light of reason. Reason, as Freud saw it, cannot always guide the chariot drawn by passion, for these violent steeds turn on one another and in their battle the reins of reason become entangled.

Freud discovered, analyzed, and stated what those keen students of human psychology, the great playwrights and novelists, had always known. But since Freud's day, several social scientists have attempted to develop systematic theories dealing with the search for power.

(3). *People seek power,* it is often said, *because they are driven by needs, wishes, desires, and motives of which they are not fully aware.*

That some people are power-hungry by nature is an ancient view. Plato's dictatorial man, as we saw, becomes so "when his nature or his pursuits or both make him intoxicated, lustful, and mad." Modern scholars have clothed similar views in modern terms. Since Freud they have often emphasized unconscious strivings. The American political scientist Harold Lasswell suggested that the power seeker pursues power as a means of compensating for psychological deprivations suffered during childhood. Typical deprivations that engender power seeking are a lack of respect and affection at an early age, which results in low self-esteem. In childhood, or later, power seekers learn to compensate for this low estimate of self-worth by pursuing power: With power they will become important, loved, respected, admired. In Lasswell's view, power seekers do not necessarily have much insight into why they seek power; they rationalize their power seeking in terms acceptable to their conscious values and perhaps to the ideology prevailing among those with whom they identify.[25]

Taking a different tack, on the assumption that persons vary in the strength of their inner drives for seeking power, several social psychologists have developed and applied ways of measuring the "motive for power."[26]

Yet like the other approaches, interpretations of influence seeking as a by-product of unconscious motives or certain enduring predispositions

[25]Harold D. Lasswell, *Power and Personality* (New York: W. W. Norton & Co., Inc., 1948), Chap. 3, "The Political Personality." The notion of compensation for weakness later entered into the description of the "authoritarian personality." One of the characteristics of this personality type was said to be a "power complex" that comes about "when an individual is forced to submit to powers . . . with which he is not fully in sympathy" and thus "is left with a nagging sense of weakness, since to admit such weakness is to damage self-respect he makes every effort to deny it—sometimes by projecting weakness onto outgroups . . . or by using the mechanism of overcompensation, whereby he seeks to present to the world an aspect of *power and toughness.*" Nevitt Sanford, "Authoritarian Personality in Contemporary Perspective," in Jeanne N. Knutson, ed., *Handbook of Political Psychology* (San Francisco: Jossey-Bass Publishers 1973), p. 145.

[26]For a description of a measurement of "the power motive" or "the need for power" and some of its applications, see David C. McClelland, *Human Motivation* (Glenview, Ill.: Scott, Foresman and Company, 1984), Chapter 8, pp. 268–332.

rooted in the person's character or personality are not wholly convincing—at least when applied to people who actively engage in seeking to gain influence over the government of the state. Some of the major difficulties are these:

1. A person who seeks influence or power does not necessarily seek them in the Government. She may seek them in other institutions, such as business, the church, and the universities.
2. A person driven by a strong desire for power and influence may not be effective in *achieving* them since he is likely to stimulate too much dislike and distrust in others.
3. Power and influence can serve many ends. Depending on culture, society, economy, and political system, influence can be used (as Lasswell and others pointed out) to acquire fame, reverence, security, respect, affection, wealth, and many other values. Hence one may seek power and influence from many different motives, including all those discussed in this chapter and many others.
4. Finally, scant empirical evidence has been provided to show that men and women who are strongly involved in political life surrounding the Government actually do so because they are driven by the motives suggested by the theories.

It seems unlikely, then, that people who seek to gain influence over the Government of the State do so for the same reasons. There are too many different reasons, conscious and unconscious, why a person might want power and influence, and too many variations in the costs and benefits of power from one political system to another and from one time to another. Both Caligula and Abraham Lincoln sought power, yet it is highly implausible to suppose that Caligula and Lincoln were driven by the same motives.

THE POWERFUL

Not all power seekers, we have said, gain power. Why do some people gain more power and influence than others?

In principle, if one gains more influence than another (over X, with respect to Y) then we may look to two possible sources of explanation—to differences in the amount of resources used and to differences in the skill or efficiency with which the resources are applied. Some people use more resources to gain influence than others do. Some people use what resources they have more efficiently, more skillfully.

Why do some people use more resources? Presumably because they expect to "gain more" by doing so. I may "gain more" than you from a given action either because the action is "less costly" to me or because the outcome of the action is "more valuable" to me. If A has more resources than B—for example, wealth—then a given outlay is less costly for A than for B (all other things being equal) because A has to forgo fewer alternatives than B. Or, in the language of the economist, A's opportunity costs are lower.

A person of wealth and a good deal of leisure can devote sixty hours a week to nonpaying political activities at considerably lower opportunity cost than a person who has to work long hours to make a living. In short, if A has more resources than B, the opportunity costs of allocating a given amount of those resources to gaining influence are less for A than for B: A can make the same outlays as B at less opportunity cost or more outlays at the same opportunity cost. In general, then, some people *use* more resources to gain influence than others do because they have *access* to more resources. And, all other things being equal, it is reasonable to expect that people with more resources will gain more influence. To this extent, then, differences in influence and influence seeking are related to differences in objective circumstances.

However, "all other things" are not usually equal. Even if their resources were objectively identical, A might allocate more resources in order to gain influence if she placed a higher value on the results. Why might A place a higher value than B on the results of an outlay of resources to gain influence?

1. Because A might expect different results from those that B expects
2. Because, though both expect the same results, A and B use different values or different scales to appraise the results
3. Because, though they expect the same results, A feels more confident about the outcome than B does

However, A's application of more resources may not result in more influence and power if B has more skill than A. For a deft politician may accomplish more with little than a clumsy politician can accomplish with a great deal. Why then do some people have more skill in politics than others?

This is a difficult question to answer. To try to do so would carry us beyond the limits of this book. In brief, however, there are three possible causes for a difference in skill between two persons, whatever the skill may be, whether walking a tightrope over the Niagara, playing the part of Mimi in *La Bohême*, or serving as majority leader in the United States Senate. These are: (1) genetic differences; (2) differences in opportunities to learn; and (3) differences in incentives to learn. The first two are differences in situation, the third a difference in motivation.

We began this section with the question—"Why do some people gain more influence than others?" A general answer is summarized in Figure 9-2.

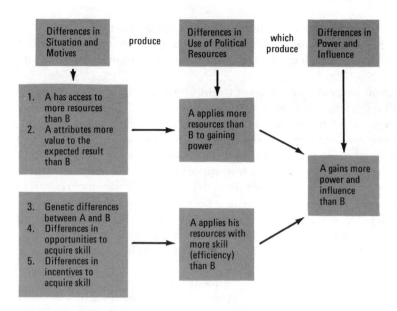

FIGURE 9-2. Why Some People Gain More Influence than Others

CHANGE AND VARIETY IN POLITICAL ORIENTATIONS

Our examination of influence seekers and the influential points up the seemingly endless variety of human motivations, incentives, orientations, and even personalities at work in political life. Attempts to impose a degree of intellectual tidiness on this disorderly array of human types have sometimes been notable for their insight and brilliance, but so far they have met with scant success. In recent years, however, social scientists have emphasized five factors that help to account for the variety of political types.

A particular person's orientations toward politics can be explained, to some degree, in the light of:

1. Personality or character
2. The general culture, or more specifically, the political culture, shared with others in the tribe, village, city, country, or world region
3. Early political orientations and how they are acquired—that is, *political socialization*
4. Personal experiences and circumstances, life situations
5. The particular situation one confronts, or believes one confronts, at a specific historical moment

Although each of these can help to make political orientations that are highly persistent—even over a person's entire adult life—each may also facilitate *changes* in orientations. For example, one's personality or character may foster open-mindness, flexibility, and receptivity to new ideas rather than closed-mindedness, rigidity, and fear of the new. So too, a culture may foster openness and flexibility rather than a rigid adherence to traditional thought and behavior. Moreover, political cultures may themselves change. While political socialization leaves a lasting imprint, like personality and culture it may help to produce flexibility, tolerance, and open-mindedness. Like them, too, patterns of political socialization may themselves change. That the last two factors may foster change is obvious.

As we observed in Chapter 6, one thing that political systems have in common is that they are subject to change. In Chapter 7 we specifically took note of the important shifts occurring in the Soviet Union and eastern European countries in the 1980s. We might have noted important shifts in other countries as well—in China, for example, or in the restoration of polyarchy in several Latin American countries. When alterations like these take place, often the most visible are the *structural* modifications—particularly in political and economic structures, as in the shift from an authoritarian regime to polyarchy or from central planning to market-oriented economies. Though more difficult to observe, it is reasonable to think that structural changes in a political system are often accompanied—and even preceded—by changes in orientations, beliefs, attitudes, or, to use a more comprehensive term, consciousness among an influential segment of the people in the system.

Some Recent Changes

As an example, in the United States the passage and subsequent vigorous enforcement of federal laws protecting the civil and political rights of black citizens—part of a profound change in structures that had long persisted with extraordinary stability—had been preceded by, and were accompanied by, changes in fundamental attitudes and beliefs among many Americans both black and white.

Another example is the alteration in values among younger generations in Europe, Japan, and the United States that Ronald Inglehart calls postmaterialist. In contrast to the materialist values of older persons in these countries who gave top priority to "physical sustenance and safety," Inglehart found that younger persons placed "heavier emphasis on belonging, self-expression and the quality of life," including the natural environment. Inglehart explained the change as resulting from the prolonged period of prosperity following World War II. Thus while the previous generations matured and acquired their values during times of scarcity and insecurity, persons born after World War II grew up in a time of relative abundance and security that encouraged the development and expression of the newer values.[27]

[27]Inglehart first reported his findings and theory in "The Silent Revolution in Europe: Intergenerational Change in Post-Industrial Societies." *American Political Science Review* 65, no.

Women

Women provide a striking example of changes in political orientations. Throughout recorded history in all parts of the globe, women have been subject to domination by males. In English and American common law, for example, a married woman could not hold personal property: All her personal possessions were legally the property of her husband, just as, before her marriage, they were the property of her father. She could not enter into a binding contract in her own name, nor make a will. Indeed, a married woman was in many respects legally the property of her husband.

Although in Europe and the English-speaking countries the harshness of traditional legal norms, like those of the common law, were mitigated in the eighteenth and nineteenth centuries by changes in legislation or interpretions, at the beginning of the twentieth century women continued to suffer from discrimination, supported by law and practice, in many different ways. As late as 1901 a Justice of the United States Supreme Court ruled that "to commit adultery with a man's wife, even with her consent . . . was an injury to his 'personal rights and property rights.'"[28]

Even after all the other institutions of polyarchy came to be fully established in more and more countries, women continued to be denied full citizenship—notably in the right to vote and to serve in public offices. As we saw in Chapter 7, democratic polyarchies were in fact male (in the United States, white male) polyarchies. Even famous advocates of democratic and republican government rejected (or simply ignored) claims that women should be full citizens. For the most part, they adopted the prevailing view that the proper role of women was marriage, procreation, and family, not politics. Thus, although John Locke held that "all men are by nature equal," he never recommended that women be allowed to vote, and considered it more or less as self-evident that in family matters the husband must have the final say.[29] Jean Jacques Rousseau, who is sometimes interpreted as radically democratic and egalitarian, announced to women (ironi-

---

4 (December 1971), pp. 991–1017, and *The Silent Revolution: Changing Values and Political Styles Among Western Publics* (Princeton, N.J.: Princeton University Press, 1977). He found that later surveys confirmed the trend even though economic growth had slowed: cf. "Post-Materialism in an Enviornment of Insecurity," *American Political Science Review* 75 (December 1981), pp. 880–900 and *Cultural Shift in Advanced Industrial Society* (Princeton, N.J.: Princeton University Press, 1989).

[28]*Tinker* v. *Colwell*, 193 U.S. 473, 481 (1904), cited in Rogers Smith, "'One United People': Second Class Female Citizenship and the American Quest for Community," *Yale Journal of the Low and the Humanities* 1, no. 2 (May 1989) 229–93, at p. 269.

[29]"[T]he husband and wife, though they have but one common concern, yet having different understandings, will unavoidably sometimes have different wills too; it therefore being necessary, that the last determination, *i.e.* the rule, should be placed somewhere, it naturally falls to the man's share, as the abler and stronger." John Locke, *The Second Treatise*, in *Two Treatises of Government* (1690), Peter Laslett, ed. (Cambridge, England: Cambridge University Press, 1970), p. 339 (par. 82). For his assertion "that all men are by nature equal," see par. 54, p. 322, and par. 4, p. 287.

cally it was in a dedication for an essay on the origin of inequality among men) that "the lot of your sex will always be to govern ours"—but only as wives and mothers, not as citizens.[30] While the Declaration of Independence asserted confidently that all men are created equal, its principal author, Thomas Jefferson "claimed that women must always be excluded from public deliberations and offices, for 'deprivation of morals' would result if they should 'mix promiscuously in gatherings of men.'"[31]

Although it is impossible to trace the historical origins of male domination, one highly plausible explanation is to be found in physical differences. Men are on average heavier, taller, and physically stronger than women and thus more capable than women of enforcing their will through physical violence and the threat of violence. Moreover, women's role in bearing and nursing children increases their vulnerability. Once established, the subjection of women was further enforced by custom, tradition, practice, and belief. But in addition to direct violence, the threat of violence, custom, and beliefs, the subjection of women was, as we just saw, backed up by law, behind which stood the coercive force of the state.

Even psychologists and psychiatrists (who for generations were mostly men) adopted and thereby reinforced a male interpretation of women. Eminent theorists like Sigmund Freud, Jean Piaget, and Erik Erikson fell "into the same observational bias. Implicitly adopting the male life as the norm, they have tried to fashion women out of a masculine cloth." Thus in formulating their theories of human development, either they gave little or no systematic attention to females or interpreted female development as essentially a deviation from the male model.[32]

What is surprising, perhaps, is that some women openly advocated change. Their opposition serves to remind us of the observation in Chapter 5 that a reigning ideology—and male domination was surely a reigning ideology virtually everywhere—is rarely if ever accepted by all members of a political system and may indeed be rejected by some. In 1792 an Englishwoman, Mary Wollstonecraft, wrote *A Vindication of the Rights of Women*. In the United States, women took an active part in the antislavery movement and concluded that their own rights also needed protection. In 1848 Elizabeth Cady Stanton and Lucretia Mott called a convention on women's rights, and soon thereafter their cause was joined by women suffragists, notably Lucy Stone and Susan B. Anthony. In England Emmeline Pankhurst formed the first women's suffrage committee in 1865. Although advocates of equal political rights for women were often met with scorn and derision for their "unfeminine" behavior and occasionally with brutal treatment by police,

---

[30]*Discourse on the Origin of Inequality* (1754) in Jean Jacques Rousseau, *On the Social Contract, Discourse on the Origin of Inequality, Discourse on Political Economy*, (Indianapolis, Ind.: Hackett Publishing Co., 1983), pp. 111–12.

[31]Cited in Smith, "One United People," p. 31.

[32]Carol Gilligan, *In A Different Voice: Psychological Theory and Women's Development* (Cambridge, Mass.: Harvard University Press, 1982), pp. 6ff.

they helped to bring about the legal (and sometimes constitutional) changes that, as we saw in Chapter 7, resulted in equal suffrage and other political rights for women in all democratic countries.

Having the same political rights as men did not mean, however, that women automatically gained equal influence with men in political and economic life or that their differences in political orientations vanished. As we saw earlier, the level of political activity tended to be lower among women than men. Whether because of discrimination, women's own attitudes, family responsibilities, or all of these, in countries with MDP societies, men continued to outnumber women in the labor force (women performing unpaid housework were not counted as part of the labor force or as gainfully employed), in years of formal education, in business and professional life, and in positions of greater prestige, income, and influence, including elective offices. And while there were notable exceptions, relatively few women (and fewer men) raised their voices in protest. Superficially at least, it was as if once the legal discrimination in political rights was brought to an end, women largely accepted as "natural" the other differences in their opportunities.

Beginning in the 1960s and with increasing strength in the following decades, however, more and more women came to view these kinds of differences in opportunities not as just and inevitable but as unjust and remediable. In the United States particularly, women's movements undertook to change practices like these and to change women's attitudes about themselves and society.[33] "Consciousness raising" in exclusively female groups without the potentially threatening presence of men became a technique for helping women to discover and develop new orientations.[34]

Meanwhile, women were moving in large numbers into the labor force. In many countries, their educational level also improved. In some countries, they approached or surpassed men in their level of political awareness and activity. Though still small, their numbers in positions of leadership and influence increased.[35]

Although we cannot complete here the account of a shift in conscious-

---

[33]A work of extraordinary influence, however, was by a French writer, Simone de Beauvoir. Her book *The Second Sex,* published in France in 1949, was published in 1953 in the United States (H. P. Parsley, trans. and ed., New York: Knopf), where it gained enormous acclaim. It was followed ten years later by the book that became for a time the fundamental text of the newly emerging American feminist movement: Betty Friedan's *The Feminine Mystique* (New York: Norton, 1963)

[34]For a description, see Catharine A. Mackinnon, *Toward a Feminist Theory of the State* (Cambridge, Mass.: Harvard University Press, 1989), Chapter 5, "Consciousness Raising," pp. 83–105.

[35]The changes were highly uneven among different countries. In the United States in 1940, 27 percent of females 14 years old and over were in the labor force; in 1987, 55 percent 16 years and over were. The educational level of women in the United States rose along with that of men: In 1986 24 percent of males 25 years or over had completed four or more years of college, and 16 percent of females had done so. However, in 1986 women accounted for 94 percent of nurses, 73 percent of teachers (except in colleges and universities), 85 percent of

ness that is far from ended, that change together with the others mentioned earlier suggests these conclusions:

1. Changes in fundamental, long-lasting, and seemingly rock-firm political orientations do occur, and sometimes they manifest themselves with astonishing swiftness.
2. These changes can often be satisfactorily explained after the fact by examining the five factors mentioned at the beginning of this section.
3. Contemporaries rarely foresee the nature of the fundamental changes in political orientations that are about to occur, or they fail to predict their timing, their extent and strength, how and when they will die down, and their consequences for policies and structure.

That further fundamental changes in political orientations will come about among people in the United States and other countries within the lifetime of the readers of this book seems certain. But what those changes will be, where, and when, we can only guess.

---

waiters and waitresses, and 85 percent of librarians but only 37 percent of executive, administrative, and managerial persons, 17 percent of physicians, 4 percent of dentists, and 36 percent of college and university teachers. The median weekly earnings for full-time wage and salary workers in 1986 was $419 for males and $290 for females. In 1984 among persons of voting age, 69 percent of women were registered and 61 percent voted in the presidential election, compared with 67 percent and 59 percent, respectively of men. However, in 1987 only 23 of 435 members of the House of Representatives were women, and 2 of 100 Senators. Among 21 industrial societies, the percentage of women who reportedly discussed politics was 77 percent in Finland, 72 percent in the United States, 60 percent in Britain, 47 percent in Italy, and 35 percent in Japan. Among sixteen European countries, women comprised 35 percent of the members of the lower house of parliament in Norway, 30 percent in Finland, 12 percent in Switzerland, 4 percent in France, and 3 percent in Britain (where, however, the prime minister was a women). See U.S. Bureau of the Census, Statistical Abstract of the United States: 1988, 108th ed. (Washington, D.C.: U.S. Government Printing Office, 1987), Tables 201, p. 125; 409, p. 244; 418, p. 249; 608, p. 366; 627, p. 376; 651, p. 394; 653, p. 395; Inglehart, *Culture Shift*, Table 1.3 and Figure 1-7, pp. 000.

TEN
POLITICAL EVALUATION

Chances are that like most readers of this book you believe that democracy is better than dictatorship. Is a belief like this exactly equivalent to saying that you like coffee better than tea? If so, your political decisions would not allow for much rational defense. Is this unavoidable? And if your political beliefs are inherently nonrational, isn't it a waste of time trying to act wisely in politics? Isn't a decision based on complete ignorance as justifiable, in the end, as one based on knowledge? If no one knew how to build a foundation and supporting structure strong enough to hold up a house, it would be foolish for anyone to try tó live in a house; we would all be better off living in tents instead. Are political beliefs, no matter how carefully constructed, pretty much like a house without foundations or supporting structures strong enough to hold them up?

In considering questions such as these it is obvious that we must move toward a much more explicitly normative orientation than in the earlier chapters. These were concerned mainly with clarifying the meaning of terms, as in Chapters 1 and 3; description, as in Chapters 2, 5, and 6; explanation, as in Chapters 4 and 7; or several of these, as in Chapters 7 and 8, which combine clarifying terms, description, and explanation. These are familiar ways of interpreting and understanding the world in daily life and ordinary discourse as well as in the natural, medical, and social or human sciences.

Chapter 4, however, explicitly introduced another equally fundamental way of interpreting and understanding the world: as a place inhabited by human beings who make judgments about better and worse—moral, ethical, normative judgments and evaluations. Not only do the different forms of influence and power invite evaluations, but the distinctions among the different forms themselves—rational persuasion and manipulated persuasion, for example, or coercive and noncoercive influence—are important to us because we evaluate different forms of influence as better and worse. So, too, with differences in political systems. We distinguish democratic from nondemocratic political systems, and polyarchies from nonpolyarchies, primarily because we believe these differences matter. Thus evaluations provide reasons for us to make some of the distinctions we do in political analysis, and to want to describe and explain how certain kinds of behavior, actions, beliefs, and systems come about.

But this takes us right back to the questions with which we began this chapter. What reasonable grounds have we for believing that one thing is better than another? That democracy, for example, is better than dictatorship?

THE PROBLEM OF VALUES IN POLITICAL PHILOSOPHY

Find me a lever long enough and a point to put it on, Archimedes is supposed to have said, and I can move the world. One of the most stubborn philosophical problems of the twentieth century has been to find what the philosopher John Rawls has called an Archimedean point on which to rest the lever of political philosophy; that is, a rational justification for moral judgments.[1]

A distinctive contribution of political philosophy had been its special attention to beliefs about values, norms, standards. Until the nineteenth century, philosophers (like other people) tended to believe that moral ideas could be about as objective and certain as empirical knowledge, because they were ultimately based on divine revelation, nature, or self-evident intuitions. But since the latter part of the nineteenth century and increasingly in the twentieth, many philosophers, and probably large sections of the political stratum in all modern societies, have taken a more subjective view. In the extreme case, as we shall see, they have asserted that no belief about

---

[1]Reprinted by permission of the publishers from *A Theory of Justice* by John Rawls, Cambridge, Mass.: The Belknap Press of Harvard University Press, copyright © 1971 by the President and Fellows of Harvard College. Some philosophers, undoubtedly a minority, contend that there is nothing about philosophy or philosophers that gives them specially privileged access to truth and thus to knowing about the "foundations" of knowledge, whether of morals, metaphysics, or anything else. In Rorty's view, for example, philosophers can, like the later Wittgenstein, "edify," but they cannot discover special truths about the foundations of knowledge. The aim of philosophers should therefore simply be to contribute to the "conversation" about significant matters, and to keep the conversation going. Richard Rorty, *Philosophy and the Mirror of Nature* (Princeton, N.J.: Princeton University Press, 1979).

any value standard can ever be rationally justified. In this perspective your saying that you believe freedom is better than slavery is no more objective than your saying that you like coffee better than tea.

The growth of "subjectivist" views is attributable to a number of factors. For one thing, a general decline in religious faith from the eighteenth century onward meant that values could no longer be successfully justified by basing them on divinely revealed religious truths. John Locke (1632–1704), whose work profoundly influenced American thinking at the time of the American Revolution and Constitutional Convention, could argue that "all men are by nature equal" because we are all equally God's children. But two centuries later, his premise was generally believed among philosophers to be too shaky to sustain his assertion. In addition, the triumphant progress of science made nonscientific knowledge look pale by comparison. In fact, a philosophical view that *only* scientific knowledge could lay claim to any objectivity gained ground. The French mathematician and philosopher Auguste Comte (1798–1857) contended that human history progressed through three stages, the religious, the metaphysical, and the scientific. Henceforth, the "positive" sciences would be the foundation for politics, ethics, law, and even religion itself. *Positivism,* as his view was named, reappeared independently in Vienna in the 1920s in an intellectual movement variously called logical positivism, neo-positivism, logical empiricism, or scientific empiricism. Although neo-positivism was primarily a philosophical interpretation of the fundamental nature of scientific knowledge, its followers tended to dismiss moral statements as meaningless. In 1936 a young Oxford don, A. J. Ayer, boldly asserted that since, unlike scientific statements, the truth of moral judgments could not be verified, moral statements were devoid of meaning.[2] But if moral assertions are meaningless—or at any rate without rational or (as neo-positivists sometimes said) "cognitive" meaning—then the moral foundations of political philosophy must also be meaningless. And if its moral foundations are inherently meaningless, then political philosophy must be a futile undertaking.

Another current of thought that deepened the problem was the view that all philosophical thought (in some versions, all thought of every kind, including the natural sciences) is determined by causes outside the consciousness and beyond the control of those who espouse it. In *deterministic* accounts, the external causes were variously ascribed to a person's particular historical period, culture, class, interests, and psychological developments.[3] If one's philosophical perspective is ultimately nothing more than a by-product of nonrational factors like these, then the attempt to create

---

[2] A. J. Ayer, *Language, Truth and Logic* (London: Gollancz, 1936; and New York: Holt, Rinehart & Winston, 1973), pp. 226–7.

[3] The view that human consciousness and actions are fully determined by external factors is generally called *determinism.* An argument for determinism because of psychological factors is presented by the psychologist B. F. Skinner in *Beyond Freedom and Dignity* (New York:

political philosophy, or for that matter even to discuss it seriously, once again seems pretty unpromising.

COUNTERTRENDS

Objections like these to the possibility that political philosophy could be a rational or even reasonable undertaking did not, however, prove to be lethal. For one thing, intelligent and thoughtful people, including political scientists and philosophers, continued to present and discuss political ideas with the utmost seriousness, and in doing so appeared to believe that their discussions were not purposeless or irrational, no matter what neo-positivists, determinists, historicists, or others might say. Serious concern for political ideas, and thus for some of the fundamental questions of moral and political philosophy, was undoubtedly stimulated by the upheavals of the twentieth century. Two world wars and innumerable smaller ones, the worldwide economic depression of the 1930s, revolution, the breakdown of democracy in several countries, the use and expansion of nuclear weapons, the prospect of nuclear annihilation, the American urban riots of the 1960s, the Vietnam War, Watergate, the near-impeachment and resignation of President Nixon—even among Americans these and other events weakened many of the more comfortable and optimistic beliefs of an earlier time and may have stimulated an interest in some of the fundamental questions posed by political philosophers.[4]

Moreover, the influence of neo-positivism peaked and, as often happens with philosophical movements, rapidly waned. In 1977 A. J. Ayer lamented that he had gone from being a Young Turk to old hat without an

---

Alfred A. Knopf, Inc., 1971). See also *Walden Two* (New York: MacMillan, Inc., 1948) and Finley Carpenter, *The Skinner Primer* (New York: Free Press, 1974). The term *relativism* is often applied to the argument that different factors produce different and even conflicting but equally justifiable ways of understanding, interpreting, and explaining the world among different individuals and different groups. A common form of relativism, particularly among anthropologists, is *cultural* relativism. When applied to morality, such views become *moral relativism*. *Historicism* is a term often applied to historians or others who contend that political (or other) thought can be more or less fully explained and interpreted as a by-product of assumptions grounded in the writer's historical period. Arguments for an historicist view may be found in Quentin Skinner, "Meaning and Understanding in the History of Ideas," *History and Theory* 8 (1969): 3–53 and "Some Problems in the Analysis of Political Thought and Action," *Political Theory* 2 (1974): 277–303. A special and important form of historicism has been the *historical determinism* of Marx and his followers. For a recent interpretation, see G. A. Cohen, *Karl Marx: Theory of History* (Princeton, N.J.: Princeton University Press, 1978).

[4] In a famous aphorism, the philosopher Georg Wilhelm Friedrich Hegel (1770–1831) remarked that the owl of Minerva flies at dusk, by which he meant that philosophy flourished not during the vigorous youth of a civilization when its norms were acted on without much questioning, but during periods of decline when the norms, now no longer seeming appropriate, underwent questioning.

intervening period of solid respectability.[5] It became obvious, too, that the philosophical void could not be filled by purely deterministic accounts.[6]

Analysis of Meaning

Some philosophers, particularly in English-speaking countries, came to believe that a satisfactory foundation for reasoning about the normative questions in political philosophy might be found in *language,* by analyzing the *meaning* we give to words and concepts in ordinary usage. The analysis of meanings in moral and political evaluation is strongly influenced by the later work of the philosopher Ludwig Wittgenstein (1889–1951).[7] In general, "analytic" or "linguistic" philosophy seeks the meaning of terms as these are actually used in ordinary, nonphilosophical language. As a result of reflecting on how we express our meaning when we wish to indicate moral and evaluative judgments, as distinguished from judgments about matters in the domain of empirical science, some writers have concluded that language is in effect divided into different "regions." The languages of different "regions" deal with different matters. The language of one region is often inappropriate and confusing when it is applied to matters requiring a rather different sort of language.

One such region, it has been argued, is moral discourse.[8] To rely exclusively on the language of the empirical sciences to explore the domain of moral discourse (as, it is argued, some noncognitivists propose to do) is fundamentally as absurd as using the language of physics or chemistry in order to discuss the esthetic qualities of a painting. One aim of the approach—with some practitioners, the exclusive aim—is to enrich and clarify moral discourse and political evaluation by heightening our understanding of the language we use when we discuss moral questions, as practically everybody does.

[5] Quoted in Brian Barry, "And Who Is My Neighbor?" *The Yale Law Journal* 88:629 (1979), 629–58, at p. 631, from Ayer's autobiography, *A Part of My Life* (London: Oxford University Press, 1977), pp. 294–95.

[6] As Deborah Baumgold remarks of historicism, "Not surprisingly, the historicist approach ... tends to dissolve the political interest of the classic texts." Her essay, "Political Commentary on the History of Political Theory," *American Political Science Review* 75:4 (December 1981), pp. 928–40, is a useful description and critique of several recent approaches to political philosophy.

[7] Wittgenstein's later work is somewhat at odds with his earlier work, which strongly influenced logical positivism. For an account of his work, see David Pears, *Ludwig Wittgenstein* (New York: The Viking Press, 1969, 1970).

[8] Hanna Fenichel Pitkin, *Wittgenstein and Justice* (Berkeley, Calif.: University of California Press, 1972). Although less directly influenced by Wittgenstein, Brian Barry, *Political Argument* (New York: Humanities Press, Inc., 1967) also stresses and exemplifies the possibilities of clarifying political judgments through (in part) the meticulous analysis of meaning. Wittgenstein's work also plays an important role in Peter Winch's critique of the social sciences, *The Idea of a Social Science and Its Relation to Philosophy* (New York: Humanities Press, 1958).

As an approach to the restoration of moral and political philosophy, however, linguistic analysis soon revealed its own shortcomings. Perhaps the most important was its failure to show convincingly how the analysis of meaning could avoid what earlier philosophers had called the *naturalistic fallacy:* the attempt to derive a statement about what we *ought* to do from statements about what *is.* Even if it were possible to show what we mean by the term "justice" in certain contexts, it would not appear to follow that we *ought* to act justly. Moreover, no analytic philosopher actually produced a work in political philosophy so powerful and convincing as to demonstrate the success of the approach. Finally, analyzing the meaning of terms often became so tedious, trivial, or arcane that no one except professional philosophers could follow the discussion, or cared to.[9]

RATIONAL CONSENSUS: HABERMAS

The discussion of the desirability of rational persuasion in Chapter 4 suggests the possibility that an Archimedean point might be found if it could be shown that people placed in a situation where only rational persuasion were permitted would agree on certain values. Their agreement might be likened to a contract among them to abide by these values. Perhaps the most influential countertrend to subjectivism and relativism has been work along these lines. Though it is impossible to provide more than very brief and incomplete sketches here, I want to mention two such approaches.[10]

In a series of works since 1970,[11] the German philosopher Jürgen Hab-

---

[9]"So far has the pendulum swung to the other extreme that I cannot remember when I last read a discussion about the criteria for a good cactus or an extra-fancy apple." Barry, "And Who Is My Neighbor?" p. 632.

[10]A third influential example is provided by David Gauthier, *Morals by Agreement* (Oxford: Clarendon Press, 1986). Gauthier seeks to "develop a theory of morals as a part of the theory of rational choice." He argues "that the rational principles for making choices, or decisions among possible actions, include some that constrain the actor pursuing his own interest in an impartial way. These we identify as moral principles." (2-3) Although Gauthier's argument is too abstract and difficult to summarize here, it is important to note that by assumption his theory excludes from consideration situations where the parties are grossly unequal at the outset. "Among unequals, one party may benefit most by coercing the other, and on our theory would have no reason to refrain." (17) Although Gauthier provides a further justification for assuming that the initial position of the parties to an agreement is non-coercive (pp. 192-97), considering the prominence of initial inequalities and coercion in political life, this would seem to be a drastic limitation on the scope of the theory. In constructing his argument as part of the theory of rational choice, however, Gauthier builds on one of the most rapidly growing approaches to political and economic analysis. Rational choice theory is also referred to as the theory of social choice, and sometimes as political economy. The literature is immense and in considerable part mathematical.

[11]A sympathetic analysis in English of Habermas's work is Thomas McCarthy, *The Critical Theory of Jürgen Habermas* (Cambridge: The MIT Press, 1978) from which the exerpts below are taken (pp. 306-7, 314).

ermas has proposed that a rational consensus on questions of truth and morals could be arrived at by discourse in an "ideal speech situation." In an ideal speech situation, the conditions "must ensure not only unlimited discussion but discussion that is free from distorting influences, whether their source be open domination, conscious strategic behavior, or the more subtle barriers to communication deriving from self-deception." The participants must have the same chance "to express their attitudes, feelings, intentions, and so on so that the participants can be truthful," and they must have sufficiently equal standing so that "the formal equality of chances to initiate and pursue communication can in fact be practiced."

Habermas would, in principle, apply the requirements of consensus reached in an ideal speech situation to both empirical and moral judgments. Empirical questions—the descriptions and explanations of earlier chapters, for example—require "theoretical discourse" leading to judgments about truth. Moral questions require "practical discourse" leading to judgments about "rightness"—i.e., moral judgments.

If all needs and interests were purely subjective, varied from person to person, and thus made consensus impossible, then of course Habermas's approach would not provide an Archimedean point and the problem of finding a rational justification for moral judgments would remain unsolved. But Habermas argues "that there are not only particular interests but common or 'generalizable' interests; and it is precisely the function of practical discourse to test which interests are capable of being 'communicatively shared,' (admit of consensus) and which are not (admit at best of a negotiated compromise). In the former case, . . . then it is a rationally motivated consensus."

The difficulties with Habermas's solution are at least two. First, the ideal speech situation is, as he admits, an ideal rarely if ever achieved in the real world. Second, as a consequence, we are left with little or nothing in the way of moral judgments that come even close to measuring up to the requirements imposed by his rigorous ideal test. In Habermas's own work we search in vain for moral judgments that are justified as a product of a rational consensus in a free speech situation.

JUSTICE BY CONTRACT: RAWLS

In 1971, John Rawls, a Harvard philosopher, published his long-awaited *A Theory of Justice.*[12] His work was immediately recognized in English-speaking countries as a fundamental contribution to political philosophy. It stimulated an unprecedented outpouring of articles, even entire books, interpret-

---

[12]See footnote 1, this chapter.

ing, supporting, or, as is usual among scholars, attacking Rawls's argument.[13] Some critics who rejected his theory or important parts of it nonetheless used it as a point of departure to develop alternate views. Throughout the following decade works appeared almost annually that grappled directly with some major question in political philosophy and attempted to set forth a solution. It is too early to say whether all this signifies a long-run revival in political philosophy or is only a blip on the radar screen of intellectual history. Meanwhile, however, the normative orientation has become a rapidly expanding frontier of political science, just as empirical analysis had become earlier. Fortunately, the revival of political philosophy need not impede the continuing growth of empirical analysis, and may even strengthen it by suggesting criteria that will help empirical investigators to judge the relative importance of questions they might undertake study.

Rawls's Argument

Rawls's argument reflects his belief in the validity of one of two fundamental *types* of moral reasoning. He proposes a *procedure* for arriving at principles of this type. And he presents two *principles of justice* that he claims to justify by means of the procedure.

Two types of moral reasoning.   One common form of moral reasoning is based exclusively on an estimate of the net sum of value of alternative *consequences*, arrived at by summing up the gains and losses for each person: as, for example, in the principle that the best rule of public policy is to seek "the greatest good of the greatest number." For obvious reasons this kind of moral reasoning is called *consequentialist*. The consequences must be evaluated, of course, against some standard of what is good or desirable. Familiar standards are happiness, pleasure, satisfaction, utility, and the like. An argument using standards like these is generally called *utilitarian*. Utilitarians typically hold that the best policy is one that *maximizes* some chosen value—happiness, utility, interests, or whatever.[14] From its inception, mod-

---

[13]For example, Brian Barry, *The Liberal Theory of Justice* (Oxford, England: Clarendon Press, 1973); and Robert Paul Wolff, *Understanding Rawls* (Princeton, N.J.: Princeton University Press, 1977). See also the articles devoted to Rawls in *The American Political Science Review*, 69:2 (June 1975).

[14]Thus in *Morals by Agreement*, Gauthier adopts the assumption that persons act rationally if and only if they seek to maximize their greatest interest or benefit (p. 7). One problem in maximizing schemes, and thus in utilitarianism, is whether to maximize the total sum of value, or the average. Classical utilitarians specified that the total sum of value ought to be maximized. But suppose a country could choose between (1) doubling its population and increasing GNP by 20 percent or (2) keeping both population and GNP the same. Maximizing the total sum would require the first policy, even though the average person's share would be reduced by 60 percent. Modern utilitarians have therefore advocated maximizing average utility, which would lead to the second policy. See the discussion in Rawls, pp. 161 ff. Of course GNP is not necessarily equivalent to happiness, pleasure, satisfaction, utility, or any other reasonable

ern economics has taken the validity of utilitarian reasoning for granted, even though the concept of utility in economics has become so abstract and disembodied that it is now only a ghostly wraith of its earlier robust life in the form of happiness or pleasure. Many of our judgments about public policies are based on utilitarian considerations. We try to estimate the gains and costs to different persons or groups in society and arrive at a judgment favoring the policy with the greatest net gain for the entire aggregate. In fact, it is difficult to see how you could make a sensible judgment about public policies if you were absolutely forbidden to employ utilitarian reasoning.

In his theory of justice, however, Rawls explicitly rejects utilitarian reasoning.[15] Instead, he grounds his theory in another familiar notion: Most of us believe some things are right, good, or just even though they might not, for example, produce the greatest happiness for the greatest number. Thus, if people have inalienable, inviolable, natural rights, then such a right should never be overridden by a mere summing up of the net utility, pleasure, or happiness of others. If people have an inviolable right to fair trial, they ought not to be deprived of that right simply because of the pleasure that convicting them might give to others, whether an aroused mob in search of a victim for lynching, a legislature wanting to ensure the conviction of an unpopular group of dissenters, or, for that matter, a majority of citizens. As Rawls says, "Justice denies that the loss of freedom for some is made right by a greater good shared by others."[16] In contrast to utilitarian reasoning, Rawls's insistence on the absolute priority of certain principles of justice reflects what Barry calls "absolutism"[17] and Rawls, "deontological" moral theory.[18]

Rawls was hardly the first to criticize utilitarian reasoning. If he made a bigger splash in political philosophy than previous critics, it was probably

---

standard of goodness. But that points to another problem of utilitarianism: how to estimate the relative value of the alternatives.

[15]Rawls, *Theory of Justice,* pp. 22–27 and 150–92.

[16]*Ibid.,* p. 28.

[17]Barry, "And Who Is My Neighbor?" p. 630.

[18]Rawls defines a deontological theory as "one that either does not specify the good independently from the right, or does not interpret the right as maximizing the good." That is, in a deontological theory either (1) what is best is not some separate end like happiness but simply bringing about what is *right,* such as justice, irrespective of other ends; or (2) what is best is not determined by maximizing the attainment of some desirable end like happiness but is an absolute requirement, regardless of the total sum of, say, happiness, that might result. In rejecting utilitarianism, Rawls does not reject consequentialist arguments in general. Deontological theories such as his do not "characterize the rightness of institutions and acts independently from their consequences. All ethical doctrines worth our attention take consequences into account in judging rightness. One which did not would simply be irrational, 'crazy'" (*Theory of Justice,* p. 30). His point is that while justice obviously requires us to take consequences into account—for example, whether a fair trail is or is not a consequence of certain procedures—justice is not a matter of a net sum of individual gains and losses but is an absolute right.

because he presented both a procedure for justifying absolute principles and two relatively specific principles to boot.

Rawls's procedure.   A central difficulty in moral reasoning is how to arrive at principles that can reasonably claim to be *general* or even *universal.* Principles based only on your own self-interest may not be persuasive to anyone whose interests are opposed to yours. Rawls's procedure is intended to overcome this difficulty.

He invites you to imagine yourselves with others attempting to arrive at an original agreement, a social contract, embodying the principles of justice for the basic structure of your society. The principles are to be what you as a free and rational person, concerned to further your own interests, would accept in an initial position of equality with the others. That is, you and others are presumed to have the same rights in choosing principles; each of you can make proposals, submit reasons for their acceptance, and so on. In one of his most ingenious and controversial moves, however, Rawls proposes that you imagine yourself to be in a hypothetical situation behind "a veil of ignorance" as to your own concrete, personal, individual interests. You are to choose rules of justice as if you don't know for sure what your own situation in the new society is going to be: whether you will be advantaged or disadvantaged, rich or poor, weak or powerful, smart or slow, and so on. In this "original position," what fundamental rules would you want to put into your social contract and subsequently have reflected in your Constitution?[19] Because of your uncertainty, he argues, you will want to make sure that the rules will prevent you from being treated too severely if you should turn out to be one of the less-advantaged persons in your society. And after all, how can you be sure what the future may bring, not only for you but for other members of your family—for your children?

Two principles of justice.   In these circumstances, Rawls contends, you would adopt the following general principles of justice:

> All social values—liberty and opportunity, income and wealth, and the bases of self-respect—are to be distributed equally unless an unequal distribution of any, or all, of these values is to everyone's advantage.[20]

Rawls unpacks from this general principle two principles of justice: The first guarantees full equality of political rights as citizens in a democratic order. The second guarantees fair (though not necessarily perfectly equal) treatment in the distribution of social and economic values.

[19]*Ibid.,* pp. 11–22. I have ignored two other important and highly controversial aspects of Rawls's procedures, his notion of reflective equilibrium (pp. 48–51), briefly discussed below in footnote 26. p. 131 and his adoption of a maximin strategy (pp. 151–56).

[20]*Ibid.,* p. 62.

First, then, each person is to have an equal right to the most extensive basic liberty compatible with a similar liberty for others.

> The basic liberties of citizens are, roughly speaking, political liberty (the right to vote and to be eligible for public office) together with freedom of speech and assembly; liberty of conscience and freedom of thought; freedom of the person, along with the right to hold (personal) property; and freedom from arbitrary arrest and seizure as defined by the concept of the rule of law. These liberties are all required to be equal by the first principle, since citizens of a just society are to have the same basic rights.[21]

Thus Rawls's first principle establishes the fundamental rights of citizenship in a liberal democratic political order. And it takes absolute priority over the second principle: "A departure from the institutions of equal liberty required by the first principle cannot be justified by, or compensated for, by greater social and economic advantages."[22]

Nonetheless, Rawls's second principle goes well beyond prevailing policies in democratic countries: Social and economic inequalities are not to be permitted except under two conditions: the inequalities are to be the benefit of *everyone* in the society, and *everyone* has an equal opportunity to seek the positions to which unequal rewards are attached.[23] Thus, under the second principle, inequalities in wealth and income could not be justified as consequences of the right to property or differences in ability, talents, or work. Income and wealth would have to be distributed equally among citizens unless it could be shown that inequality would make everyone better off—perhaps by strengthening incentives and output so that the income of *everyone* would rise. Clearly the application of Rawls's two prinicples of justice to the United States would require a profound change in public policy.

SOME IMPLICATIONS

Although such a brief discussion necessarily does an injustice to Rawls's argument, it does suggest several conclusions.

1. The Progress of Science Has Not Eliminated Political Philosophy

It is obvious, to begin with, that the view of Comte mentioned earlier and implicitly shared by some neo-positivists—that strictly scientific analysis would replace moral and political philosophy—has simply not been borne out. Even during the dog days when Anglo-American political philoso-

---

[21]*Ibid.*, p. 62.

[22]*Ibid.*, p. 61. See also his justification for the priority of liberty, pp. 541ff.

[23]*Ibid.*, pp. 60–61 and 302–3.

phy was in the doldrums, serious discussion did take place and attempts were made to move the discussion forward by using new methods, such as the analysis of meaning practiced in analytic philosophy. In fact, probably one reason for the extraordinary attention paid to *A Theory of Justice* is that it loomed up like an oasis in the desert, and to thirsty social theorists craving a refreshing discussion, it was uncommonly welcome.

There is no evident reason why an empirical or scientific orientation need be fundamentally at odds with a normative orientation. Each would enrich the other. Without the mapping of reality produced by empirically oriented analysis, political philosophy can easily become irrelevant or simply silly. Without concern for some of the fundamental questions typically posed by political philosophers, whether ancient or contemporary, empirical analysis runs the risk of degenerating into triviality.

2. Meaningful Discussion of Moral Questions Does Take Place

If hundreds of otherwise rational scholars have seriously discussed, interpreted, analyzed, argued with, and accepted or rejected, in whole or in part, *A Theory of Justice,* then it seems rather arbitrary and dogmatic to contend that a theory like Rawls's is meaningless, necessarily lacks "cognitive" meaning, is inherently incapable of rational justification, and thus lies outside the bounds of reasoned discussion. For it is perfectly obvious that rational and reasonable people *do* find Rawls's theory meaningful. To be sure, they may not find it meaningful in the way that a physicist would find the statement, "Although quarks are a fundamental constituent of protons, they can neither exist in isolation nor be observed," meaningful. Of course, a theory like Rawls's may be wrong. But in principle, so might any empirical proposition, including the one about quarks.

3. Political Philosophy Is Inescapably Controversial

Nonetheless, it is extremely unlikely that any philosophical theory will ever gain the degree of consensus among experts that often develops around certain scientific theories. From its very beginnings, statements and theories in political philosopohy have been highly controversial. Socrates thrived on controversy, and Aristotle disagreed fundamentally with his teacher Plato, Socrates' most famous pupil. As I have already suggested, one of the remarkable achievements of *A Theory of Justice* is the amount of controversy it triggered. Critics have attacked virtually every part of Rawls's theory. Among other objections, critics contend that:

- It is unreasonable to give absolute priority to priniciples of justice over all utilitarian considerations.

- The veil of ignorance is too artificial, since you cannot reasonably be expected to choose principles in complete ignorance of your own future prospects.

- It is not necessarily rational to be as cautious in the face of uncertainty as Rawls believes. If you would like to gamble on your chances of coming out on top, you might reasonably want rules that would permit much greater inequality than do Rawls's two principles.

- To give absolute priority to political rights over social and economic rights is not necessarily a reasonable trade-off, except perhaps in wealthy countries.[24]

- The second principle would forbid adopting any policy under which the worst off would gain nothing, or suffer an ever-so-slight loss, even if many slightly better-off people would gain a great deal. This seems utterly unreasonable.

- And so on.

Since the past does not invariably foretell the future, the fact that political philosophy has been extremely controversial from time of Socrates, through Rawls's time, to yesterday does not guarantee that it will always be so. Adherents to a particular philosophy or ideology often seem to believe that their own views are so reasonable that no reasonable person could, on understanding them, disagree. Consequently the hope never dies that a particular philosophical or ideological perspective—usually one's own, of course—will in time gain universal endorsement.

Yet the fact that the historical record is one of disagreement and controversy is surely no accident. There are, in fact, powerful reasons for believing that no specific political philosophy is ever likely to command general agreement among political philosophers, social theorists, political leaders, ideologues, activists, and ordinary citizens— at least in places where opportunities exist for relatively free discussion.

How decide the truth of philosophical theories?   For one thing, to prescribe how the truth of a philosophical theory is to be decided is itself a difficult, highly controversial question. To be sure, in the natural sciences the relations among theory, experiment, and reality are far more complex

---

[24]Rawls assumes a "condition of moderate scarcity" in which "natural and other resources are not so abundant that schemes of cooperation become superfluous, nor are conditions so harsh that fruitful ventures must *inevitably* break down" (p. 127, 257). Since it is unlikely that "fruitful ventures must *inevitably* break down" in any society, literally interpreted Rawls's condition of moderate scarcity would exist even in Bangladesh, and thus practically everywhere in the world. Clearly, however, Rawls does not mean his words to be interpreted literally at this point. Only as he approaches the end of his long book does Rawls explain *why* he assigns priority to liberty: "[A]s the conditions of civilization improve, the marginal significance for our own good of further economic and social advantages diminishes relative to the interests of liberty ..." because "as the general level of well-being rises ... only the less urgent wants remain to be met by further advances" while the advantages of liberty increase (pp. 542–43).

than is commonly supposed, particularly, perhaps, in the rapidly expanding field of particle physics.[25] Yet nature does have its ways—sometimes gentle, sometimes brutal—of reminding theorists of what it will tolerate as valid theoretical descriptions about it. But whether nature, or any other reality, imposes limits on the truth of moral theories, and if so how and what, are themselves sharply debated issues.[26] It is not only that moral theories themselves are highly controversial. It is as if physicists could not agree whether protons exist until they settled the philosophical question as to whether anything exists "out there" and how we can possibly know about it if it does.

Ultimate grounds? An important reason for disagreement on how we should decide about the truth of moral judgments is that people disagree about the ultimate grounds on which moral judgments are to be justified. These grounds include divine revelation, as in the Ten Commandments; authority, as in authoritatively received accounts of divine revelations, such as the Bible or the Koran, and subsequent interpretations of these accounts given by rabbis, priests, religious leaders, mullahs, monks, etc.; awareness produced by holistic or mystical union with the cosmos in an extraordinary state of consciousness; intuition; feelings; personal or general experiences; the "common sense of mankind"; and reason. Someone who justifies a moral judgment on one of these grounds is not likely to convince you of its validity if you happen to believe such judgments can be justified only on some different ground.

Meaning of key concepts? Because key terms in philosophical theory often refer to extremely complex concepts, language itself is frequently a barrier to agreement. Ambiguities of meaning may contribute to flatly contradictory understandings and to support for fundamentally conflicting policies. As an example, consider a concept that has played a central role in views about democracy and justice from Plato and Aristotle to Rawls and his critics: equality. What do we mean by equality?

---

[25]For an extreme example, see Bernard d'Espagnat, "The Quantum Theory and Reality," *Scientific American,* Vol 241 (November, 1979) pp. 158–81. The article is summarized as follows: "The doctrine that the world is made up of objects whose existence is independent of human consciousness turns out to be in conflict with quantum mechanics and with facts established by experiment" (p. 158).

[26]Thus Rawls advances "the notion of reflective equilibrium" as a way of testing the validity of a moral philosophy. What he means is unclear. He proposes that we reflect about alternative conceptions in a considered way, under conditions in which we are not "influenced by an excessive attention to our own interests." Under these conditions you imaginatively test out the alternative conceptions against your "sense of justice," modify your original judgments, and finally arrive at a judgment that best fits your own sense of justice (pp. 48ff.). The possibility that you may end up where you started, but with a more firmly rationalized position, is hardly to be dismissed.

"Equality is the simplest and most abstract of notions," Douglas Rae has written, "yet the practices of the world are irremediably concrete and complex.
How, imaginably, could the former govern the latter? It cannot. We are always
confronted with more than one practical meaning for equality and equality
itself cannot provide a basis for choosing among them."[27]

We cannot think clearly about equality, Rae contends, without a "grammar
of equality" that unpacks its various and often contradictory meanings. If
you are not aware of these different meanings, you can easily choose and
justify contradictory policies, all in the name of equality. Although there is
insufficient space here to present Rae's grammar in full. I want to mention
two striking examples of meanings that are fundamentally contradictory.
Equality of opportunity, Rae points out, is not one thing, it is two very different
things. Equal opportunity may be either:

- *Prospect-regarding*—each person has the same *probability* of attaining a given
  goal, such as a job or admission to a medical school; or
- *Means-regarding*—each person has the same *means* for attaining a given goal.

If you wanted to create the first kind of equal opportunity, you would try
to ensure that everyone had an equal chance to get the job or the slot in
medical school, no matter what their means or resources might be. If you
wanted to create the second, you would try to ensure that everyone had the
same means, instruments, resources, or capabilities for getting there. But as
Rae points out:

> Given strictly unequal talents, every policy of means-regarding equal opportu-
> nity must violate equality of prospects, and every prospect-regarding equal
> opportunity must violate equality of means.[28]

You simply cannot have it both ways.

Another fundamental conflict among policies arises because equality
may be either:

1. *Lot-regarding*—people are awarded identical kinds of things, or lots, or por-
   tions, or the like; or
2. *Person-regarding*—different persons are awarded things that are of equal value
   to each person, though they may not be identical in quantity.

[27]Reprinted by permission of the publishers from *Equalities* by Douglas Rae, Cambridge,
Mass.: Harvard University Press, copyright © 1981 by the President and fellows of Harvard
College.

[28]*Ibid.,* pp. 64–69. Difficulties in the idea of equal opportunity are also discussed in John
H. Schaar, "Equality of Opportunity, and Beyond," in J. Roland Pennock and John W. Chap-
man, eds. *Equality (Nomos IX).* (New York: Atherton Press, 1967), pp. 228–249.

Lot-regarding equality means identical treatment for everyone. It is lot-regarding equality to award one vote to each citizen, guarantee everyone twelve years of free schooling, or ensure that everyone between the ages of 18 and 30 has an exactly equal chance to be drafted for military service. But, as Rae points out, draftees would also receive lot-regarding equality if they were all issued size 8-D boots. Obviously it would be fairer—and much more sensible all around—not to issue identical boots to everyone but to issue each person boots that fit. This is person-regarding equality. A commonly used example is this: Suppose you have healthy kidneys and your friend, who does not, will die without regular and expensive dialysis. Identical treatment, or lot-regarding equality, would require either that you both receive dialysis, or that neither does. Obviously either policy is foolish, and the second would be deadly for your friend. In this case, a policy based on person-regarding equality would make it possible for your friend to receive dialysis, while you would not get any treatment at all.[29]

A lot-regarding policy is usually much easier to specify and apply because all you need to do is to hand out identical bundles of things—dollars, votes, chances of being drafted, or whatnot. You need only to judge whether two or more piles of things are of equal magnitude. You do not need to arrange things into heaps that may vary in size in order to have the same value for different people. The problem is, then, that although a policy based on lot-regarding equality would be easier to apply, it would often be grossly unfair, while a policy of person-regarding equality, though sometimes much fairer, would also be more difficult to apply because you must somehow determine the value things have for different persons. You might easily be tempted therefore to go along with lot-regarding equality (which, after all, is sometimes fair) or to abandon the idea of equality altogether. But if you choose the first, you will often bring about extreme injustice, while if you choose the second, you will simply be throwing in the towel.

An inescapable plurality of modern perspectives? It should not be surprising, then, that political and moral philosophy is so controversial. Although many writers, like Habermas and Rawls,[30] appear to believe that reasonable human beings should be able to reach agreement, some philosophers contend that the domain of value contains a diversity of particular values, such as freedom, equality, love, and courage, that cannot necessarily be melded into a single harmonious system. The most eminent exponent of this view was the American psychologist and philosopher William James (1842–1910), who contended that the universe of values is inescapably plu-

---

[29]Cf. the discussion in Rae, *Equalities,* Chapter 5, pp. 82–103.

[30]And Gauthier, who describes the theory of *Morals by Agreement* as "a contractarian Theory of Morals" (p. 17).

ralistic.[31] To use contemporary jargon, if the universe of values is pluralistic, then there are bound to be trade-offs among conflicting values.

More recently, Thomas Nagel has argued that values conflicts also arise because different *systems* of value may specify different courses of concrete action. He describes "five fundamental types of value that give rise to basic conflict." These are specific obligations, of the kind you have to your friends and family (whose life should you first try to save in an emergency?); utility, which we encountered earlier as the most prominent form of consequentialism; general or universal rights, as in Rawls; perfectionist values like freedom, love, dignity, respect, justice, and so on; and your commitment to carrying out your own life plans—being the person you are and want to be. These sometimes lay down conflicting requirements for your actions and policies, and in Nagel's view they are so fundamentally different that "no single, reductive method or a clear set of priorities" exists for settling conflicts among them.[32]

Extraneous influences on moral thinking?   So far I have largely ignored the possible effects of various "extraneous" influences on our moral judgments. But we cannot ignore the force of our own particular interests, our ideological commitments, the special influences of our own culture, environment, and historical period, and loyalties that, though perhaps nonrational, are necessary to the continuing existence of any community.[33] You cannot make moral judgments or adopt a political philosophy, or for that matter create one, in a complete personal, social, and historical vacuum.

---

[31]William James, *A Pluralistic Universe* (New York: Longman, Inc., 1909).

[32]Thomas Nagel, "The Fragmentation of Value," in *Mortal Questions* (Cambridge: Cambridge University Press, 1979), pp. 128–41. James S. Fishkin, in *The Limits of Obligation* (New Haven, Conn.: Yale University Press, 1982) contends that "our common ethical assumptions, which work well enough at the small scale, break down when they are applied to large enough numbers" (p. 3). He shows that when applied on a large scale, the common assumption of moral reasoning that we all have some *general* or universal obligations conflicts with two other common assumptions about moral obligations: (1) that there should be a cut-off for heroism—certain levels of sacrifice cannot morally be required of any given individual; and (2) that there is a robust zone of indifference—a substantial proportion of any person's activities fall within a zone where free personal choice is morally permissible (that is, we aren't required to do *everything* we do because of a moral obligation, which would make life a living hell).

[33]For the contrary view that among all peoples, irrespective of culture, history and so on, moral understanding, like language, spatial and temporal relations, and number, develops through certain definite *stages*, see the work of the psychologist Lawrence Kohlberg, in particular, *The Philosophy of Moral Development, Moral Stages and the Idea of Justice* (San Francisco: Harper & Row Publishers, Inc., 1981). Although most people may not reach the sixth and highest stage of universal ethical principles, everyone, Kohlberg contends, moves through the *same* stages. These begin with simply obeying rules to avoid punishment; develop to a second stage of conforming to obtain rewards, have favors returned, and so on; up to stage 5, seeing right action in terms of individual rights agreed on by the whole society; and finally, to stage 6, choosing ethical principles that are logically comprehensive, universal, and consistent, such as the Golden Rule or Kant's Categorical Imperative. For his summary of the stages, see pp. 17–20. Needless to say, the validity of Kohlberg's empirical theory is itself controversial.

DIVERSITY, CONFLICTS, REGIMES

Conflict over values—and so over political philosophies—appears to be unavoidable. That is a problem both for a person and for a political system.

As I said at the beginning of this chapter, no person can altogether avoid employing standards of value in making judgments. To say that you will refuse to make any judgments unless you can be absolutely certain about the ultimate validity of your own values is itself a moral judgment—one based, I should think, on a highly uncertain standard of value, and a bit shabby, to boot. You can, however, attempt to arrive at judgments responsibly, by trying to understand the significance and consequences of the alternatives available. Of course, if you prefer, you can also choose to act irresponsibly.

Conflicting views about values and the policies they might justify also pose problems for a political system. How should such conflicts be dealt with, and what institutions are best for dealing with them? To answer these questions responsibly would require you to circle back through the topics taken up in previous chapters: the forms of influence, your evaluation of coercion and rational persuasion, the significance of differences in political regimes, the institutions of polyarchy, its requirements and prospects, and even the political nature of human beings. Your answer would constitute your moral and political philosophy.

ELEVEN

CHOOSING POLICIES: STRATEGIES OF INQUIRY AND DECISION

Choosing a policy implies that you possess both normative standards and empirical judgments. For when you choose a policy, you are trying to move toward some goal that you believe is desirable, and you are therefore compelled to make judgments about the possible ways of reaching that goal and how easy or difficult each might be. A good policy is a path to the best situation you can reach at a cost you think it worthwhile to pay.

For reasons that previous chapters make evident, the act of adopting a policy, particularly an important policy, is nearly always surrounded by a cloud of uncertainty. We are uncertain as to matters of fact: if we elect X, what will he actually do in office? Are the policies I want more likely to be achieved through a third party than through one of the major parties? Is the society I desire more likely to be fostered by increasing participation in politics? If so, what can I do to expand participation? Would the use of violence for specific ends I favor significantly increase the chances of a repressive reaction?

We are often uncertain, too, as to matters of value: Should I support greater local control, which I favor, if it impedes another of my goals, racial integration? Is coercive violence, which I regard as intrinsically evil, ever justified—as in the American Revolution or the Civil War? If not, am I simply permitting coercive violence by others? If so, in what circumstances?

When, if ever, is intolerance of opinion or advocacy justified in a democracy?

Uncertainty over the answers to questions like these, and there are thousands of such questions, seems to be inherent in political life. What strategies of inquiry help to improve the quality of one's political decisions amid the inevitable uncertainties?

STRATEGIES OF PURE SCIENCE

There is a long-enduring and apparently irrepressible hope among students of politics that a choice among different political alternatives can be based on a pure science of politics. In earlier times, this pure science was to have included not only the factual or empirical elements, as in physics or chemistry, but also the normative or evaluational elements. In this century, however, as the term "science" increasingly has come to mean *empirical* science, the aspiration toward a pure science of politics has come to mean an empirical science of politics. According to this view, an empirical science of politics would be concerned exclusively with the validity of the factual or empirical elements. To be sure, its knowledge would be applied in action; but the validity of the ends, goals, or values sought in action would, as such, lie outside the domain of the pure science.

Some advocates of a pure science of politics share the belief of certain positivists mentioned in the last chapter that although there are scientific procedures for establishing the objective validity of empirical propositions, no procedures exist for determining the objective truth or falsity of a statement asserting that something is good or valuable. But the idea of a pure science of politics is not necessarily opposed by those who believe it is possible to arrive at objective standards of value. After all, one who believes in the value of health would probably want an empirical science of medicine that a doctor might use to cure a sick patient. So, too, one who believes that some form of equality, for example, is objectively better than inequality might advocate an empirical science of politics that would, among other things, provide reliable scientific knowledge about the conditions that facilitate or hinder attaining this equality.

Is a pure science of politics possible or desirable? Like all the other questions touched on in this chapter, this too is vigorously contested. Lack of space prevents us from exploring the major issues here.[1] Nonetheless, if only to illustrate the complexities of the argument, it may be useful to take a brief look at several of the issues.

---

[1] Cf. J. Donald Moon, "The Logic of Political Inquiry: A Synthesis of Opposed Perspectives," in *The Handbook of Political Science*, Fred I. Greenstein and Nelson W. Polsby, eds. (Reading, Mass.: Addison-Wesley Publishing Co., Inc., 1975). Further references are found on p. 148.

Can Political Phenomena Be Measured?

As everyone knows, discoveries in the natural sciences have been greatly aided by possibilities of measurement. Nature, it has been said, loves quantity. One key subject of dispute is the extent to which valid and reliable measures, comparable to those used in the natural sciences, can be developed for political phenomena.

In politics as elsewhere, it is an enormous and obvious advantage to be able to measure differences. Suppose one is wrestling with the question of what political system is best. One might then wish to know what difference it makes whether a system is a polyarchy or one of the many alternatives to polyarchy.

Consider the familiar way of analyzing experience symbolized in Figure 11-1. The paradigm is commonplace not only in the natural sciences, in medicine, and in the social and behavioral sciences but also in everyday life. In Chapter 5, we applied it to political systems; we can also apply it to political evaluation. Suppose, for example, that differences in "coercion," "conflict," or "personal freedom" are thought to be important. We may then want to know whether differences in characteristics of political systems (II) have consequences for "coercion," "conflict," or "personal freedom" (I). If they do, then we also may want to know what conditions (III) are likely to bring about or prevent the development of a "freedom-enhancing" system, or a "minimal-coercion" system, or a "peaceful-settlement" system. This kind of thinking is *causal analysis,* the attempt to understand causes. In politics, as in medicine, one wants to understand causes in order to obtain desired results, such as enhanced freedom, greater equality, more security, less coercion, greater social peace, or other goals.

But how can we find out what changes in conditions (III) produce variations in systems (II), which in turn lead to differences in consequences (I)? For self-evident reasons, politics largely excludes the possibility of experimentation in a strict sense. Fortunately, however, good logical approximations to experimentation can be made by the application of rather powerful quantitative methods—provided the data are in quantitative form. One recent innovation in political analysis—both a cause and an effect of

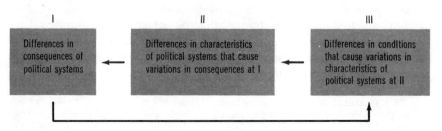

FIGURE 11-1. Analyzing Experience: A Common Paradigm

the flood of data—is a vigorous attempt to develop ways of measuring political phenomena to provide quantitative and not merely qualitative data bearing on relevant differences.

Some of the older skepticism about quantitative data was a product of rather unsophisticated ideas about measurement. Most people think of "measurement" only in terms of what specialists on measurement call *interval*-measures, like those used for height, weight, population, area, and so on. Although interval-measures are used for some phenomena relevant to differences in political systems—rates of voter turnout in elections, for example—most political phenomena are subject at best only to *ordinal* measurement, that is, a ranking according to "more," "equal," or "less." Fortunately, ranking or ordinal measurement also allows powerful quantitative methods to be used on data.

One advantage of quantitative data, then, is that they greatly facilitate causal analysis. A second advantage is that quantitative data can be much more efficiently analyzed than qualitative data, particularly with the aid of computers. Quantitative methods thus offer a possible way of coping with the flood of data about political systems that now threatens to inundate us. Although the prospect seems slight that quantitative methods will ever entirely displace the more familiar methods of qualitative analysis, it is hardly open to doubt that in the future, political analysis will make far more use of quantitative data and methods than it has in the past.[2]

When Does a Difference "Make a Difference"?

When is a difference trivial and when does it matter? One can rapidly traverse a very small circle right back to the starting point: A difference matters if one thinks that directly or indirectly it has large enough consequences for one's values. Large enough for what? Large enough to matter.

In political controversy it is not always possible to break out of this circle. What is important to one observer sometimes seems utterly trivial to another.

If disagreement as to whether a difference is trivial or important cannot *always* be settled, dispute of this kind *sometimes* can be profitably bypassed. For in practice, many people do share similar views about the relative importance of certain differences. Moreover, a solution satisfactory to all can sometimes be obtained by an analysis that takes into account *all* the differences thought to be relevant. An explanation of why different modern societies develop such varying political systems as inclusive polyarchies, competitive oligarchies, conservative authoritarian regimes, and modern-

---

[2]The subject of measurement and quantitative political analysis is vast, and the discussion here necessarily skims the surface. The topic is treated much more extensively in Edward R. Tufte, *Data Analysis for Politics and Policy* (Englewood Cliffs, N.J.: Prentice-Hall, Inc., 1974).

izing dictatorships would be important to advocates of each type of system. These considerations suggest an obvious but not trivial conclusion: With respect to any characteristic on which political systems differ, the greater the amount of variation or difference one's analysis can explain, the more useful or "powerful" the analysis is.

Yet the question remains whether "important" differences in political phenomena can be measured adequately. Clearly the utility of a science of politics depends heavily on the answer to this question. In arriving at an answer, the reader may wish to reflect on evidence contained in several of the earlier chapters in this book, particularly Chapters 6 and 7. Only a few decades ago, attempts to compare the countries of the world on a scale of democracy or polyarchy would have been regarded by most political scientists as absurd. They are still so regarded by many; but an increasing minority argue that even inadequate quantitative data are useful supplements to qualitative judgments that often rest upon highly impressionistic evidence.

Nonetheless, it would be premature to conclude that you will soon be able to make political choices on factual appraisals as solid as those in the natural sciences or engineering. There seems to be no satisfactory way to predict the rate at which factual knowledge required for political choices will increase. It is reasonable to conjecture that the flood of data now inundating us will in time be matched by an increase in verified hypotheses and theories. But the history of the natural sciences suggests that more data do not lead automatically to the discovery of nature's regularities.

Even under highly optimistic assumptions about the rate of increase in our factual knowledge, it seems quite clear that at present and in the near future a great many political choices are bound to be surrounded by a cloud of uncertainty. For in comparison with the natural sciences, medicine, or engineering, in which judgments about the value, moral quality, or goodness of different alternatives are ordinarily absent or relatively simple, in politics moral judgments are pervasive, powerful, and complex. The relative importance of a "fact," as we have seen, depends on one's standard of value.

HOLISTIC STRATEGIES

Since political choices are usually clouded by uncertainties, some students of decision making have tried to develop strategies realistically adapted to situations of limited knowledge. Their approach is best seen as a reaction to strategies of perfect rationality, sometimes called *synoptic* or *holistic* approaches, that emphasize the desirability of a complete search for a rational answer before a choice is made. What is sometimes thought to be the ideal strategy of perfect rationality has been described as follows:

1. Faced with a given problem,
2. a rational man first clarifies his goals, values, or objectives, and then ranks or otherwise organizes them in his mind;
3. he then lists all important possible ways of—policies for—achieving his goals
4. and investigates all the important consequences that would follow from each of the alternative policies.
5. at which point he is in a position to compare consequences of each policy with goals
6. and so choose the policy with consequences most closely matching his goals.[3]

This kind of strategy has great appeal—in the abstract. Yet in practice it is hardly more than a definition of perfect rationality; and perfect rationality has been unattainable, in politics as elsewhere. In practice, one is probably never in a position to acquire all the knowledge one needs for a completely rational decision on significant political questions.

Even if in practice a synoptic or holistic strategy is impossible to carry out completely, is it not, nevertheless, the ideal strategy? Even if we know we must fall short of perfect rationality, does not the synoptic strategy provide us with the model toward which we should aspire? Although the affirmative answer is tempting and plausible, in recent years critics have argued that the synoptic model is highly misleading. While it might provide a definition of perfect rationality, as a model for decision making it is generally useless or even downright harmful.

Critics of the synoptic model[4] contend that in practice decision makers rarely if ever go through the steps outlined above. Because of limitations in our knowledge, decisions are made—and *must* be made—in the midst of uncertainties. If we postponed decisions until we approached perfect rationality, we would never make a decision.

STRATEGIES OF LIMITED RATIONALITY

In practice, you can cope with uncertainty in a number of useful ways. You can search for satisfactory rather than perfect solutions to problems. You can make a tentative decision and see what happens. You can take advan-

[3]Charles E. Lindblom, *The Policy-Making Process,* 2nd ed. (Englewood Cliffs, N.J.: Prentice-Hall, Inc., 1980).

[4]A leading critic of synoptic approaches to decision making and an advocate of limited strategies is Lindblom, whose views will be found in *Ibid.,* particularly at pp. 14–27, and in D. Braybrooke and C. E. Lindblom, *A Strategy of Decision* (New York: Free Press, 1963). See also *The Intelligence of Democracy.* (New York: The Free Press, 1965). In *Politics and Markets* (New York: Basic Books, Inc., Publishers, 1977), though less enthusiastic about limited strategies, he is highly critical of the alleged rationality of comprehensive schemes of centralized planning. See esp. pp. 322–24. Another leading critic of holistic strategies is Herbert A. Simon, who has long argued that actual behavior inevitably falls far short of the requirements of models of rational

tage of feedback, or information created by the initial decision itself.[5] As a result of feedback, you can change your goals, even highly important goals. You can usually assume, too, that the decision you will make is an endless series of steps, so that your errors can be corrected as you proceed. Thus you can frequently adopt an "incrementalist" strategy: Starting with an existing state of affairs about which a good deal is known, you can make small or incremental changes in the desired direction and then see what the next steps should be. You can go on making incremental changes indefinitely. A series of incremental changes can, in time, add up to a profound transformation: If you increase anything at the rate of 5 percent a year, you will double it in fourteen years.

Strategies that aim at perfect rationality are plausible and appealing, but they seem virtually impossible to execute. Strategies that aim at limited rationality seem somehow less "rational"—yet in most situations limited strategies are all that you or anyone else will have for making decisions.

EXPERIMENTAL STRATEGIES

Troubled by the high degree of uncertainty surrounding policy making by governments, the comparatively low level of reliable knowledge on which decisions must be based, and palpable failures in policies produced both by holistic and by incremental strategies, some political analysts have begun to emphasize the possibility of reducing ignorance and uncertainty in policy making by deliberate experimentation, or small-scale tryouts prior to the adoption of policies.

Obviously not all crucial decisions can be preceded by a small-scale tryout. Foreign policies, for example, hardly lend themselves to prior experimentation. The idea also creates images of inhumane experiments with powerless victims, such as prisoners who may be coerced into participating or ill-informed subjects whose "consent" is gained by manipulative persuasion.

Proponents of experimentalism in policy making point out, however, that in practice, governments do make decisions on a variety of matters with wholly inadequate knowledge about the results to be expected. Not only are policies adopted that would be rejected if the results had been correctly foreseen; policies are also rejected that would have been adopted if the

---

behavior. He proposes a "principle of bounded rationality" as an alternative. *Models of Man* (New York: John Wiley and Sons, 1957), pp. 196ff. and *Administrative Behavior*, 2nd ed. (New York: Macmillan, 1957), pp. 80 ff. A brief and readable account is his *Reason in Human Affairs* (Stanford, Calif. Stanford University Press, 1983), especially pp. 12–35 and 75–107.

[5]See Karl W. Deutsch, *The Nerves of Government* (New York: The Free Press, 1963), Chap. Eleven, "Government as a Process of Steering: The Concepts of Feedback, Goal, and Purpose," pp. 182–199.

outcomes were better understood. Adopting or rejecting policy alternatives has favorable and harmful consequences for millions of people and costs billions of dollars in both private and public outlays. Thus policy decisions do in fact "experiment" with the welfare and happiness of people. But this experimentation is large scale, costly, and lacks all the criteria of a scientific experiment designed to produce reliable knowledge. Hence, often it would be feasible and much more reasonable, it is argued, to run small-scale, controlled, carefully studied tryouts in advance.[6]

SEARCHING FOR ALTERNATIVES

None of these strategies can guarantee that it will lead to the discovery of the best available alternatives. As in the arts, in science, in mathematics, or in the exploration of space, discovery requires an imaginative search.

There is, then, an indispensable need in political analysis for the informed imagination; for speculation, guided by knowledge, that transcends the received truths; for the design and contemplation of Utopias; for a willingness to think hard about unthinkable alternatives to all the too easily thinkable solutions. There is, in short, a need for a creative search inspired by the hunch that somewhere between the unattainable best and the kind of mediocrity so often attained in political matters there lies a universe of better alternatives—and worse ones, too—all waiting to be explored.

[6]The Brookings Institution, Washington, D.C., created a Panel on Social Experimentation to "assess the usefulness of experiments as a way of increasing knowledge about the effects of domestic social policies and programs of the federal government." Studies include Edward M. Gramlich and Patricia P. Koshel, *Educational Performance Contracting: An Evaluation of an Experiment* (1975); Joseph A. Pechman and P. Michael Timpane, eds., *Work Incentives and Income Guarantees: The New Jersey Negative Income Tax Experiment* (1975); and Alice M. Rivlin and P. Michael Timpane, eds., *Planned Variation: Should We Give Up or Try Harder?* (1975).

INDEX